Spirituality at the School Gate

Spirituality at the School Gate

The Importance of Encounter

DIANE JACKSON

Foreword by Gladys Ganiel

WIPF & STOCK · Eugene, Oregon

SPIRITUALITY AT THE SCHOOL GATE
The Importance of Encounter

Wipf & Stock
An Imprint of Wipf and Stock Publishers
199 W. 8th Ave., Suite 3
Eugene, OR 97401

www.wipfandstock.com

PAPERBACK ISBN: 978-1-7252-6427-4
HARDCOVER ISBN: 978-1-7252-6428-1
EBOOK ISBN: 978-1-7252-6429-8

Manufactured in the U.S.A.   03/30/20

This book is dedicated to mums at school gates everywhere.
You are seen and the work you are doing matters.

Contents

Foreword

In *Spirituality at the School Gate,* Diane Jackson uncovers the exceptional in the everyday, alerting us to insights that should become central to our understanding of the spirituality of motherhood and women's relationships.

Jackson makes a compelling case that women's experiences as they deposit and collect children at school gates can be sites for meaningful human (and divine) encounters. Jackson's own experience of discovering this for herself was the inspiration for her study. It motivates her to collect and compare other women's experiences, in the process alerting scholars of "everyday religion" to a site of women's spirituality that they had previously overlooked. Jackson's own honesty about her struggles to recognize the school gate as an opportunity for divine encounters gives her scholarship a rare, engaged intentionality.

Feminist scholars of religion and mothers-of-faith, regardless of whether or not those two categories overlap, have long realized that women's experiences of religion have been overlooked and undervalued. The seemingly mundane task of school gate duty, which Jackson quite accurately describes as a part-time job in and of itself, provides a locus around which women share their experiences. One of this book's most important contributions is the voice it gives to those women, in the process honoring their role in nurturing their own and their families' spiritual lives, and in passing faith on to the next generation.

Jackson acknowledges that her research is exploratory and based on a small, limited sample. But it makes valuable contributions in several areas. Studies of everyday religion in Ireland are very rare; *Spirituality at the School Gate* begins to paint a picture of the everyday spirituality of mothers from (evangelical) Protestant traditions. Likewise, studies of the role of women in religion in contemporary Ireland are limited; *Spirituality at the School Gate* reminds us that this could be a burgeoning field of study. Further, there are few studies that really seek to understand how Christianity is surviving in a rapidly secularizing Ireland; *Spirituality at the School Gate* gives us new perspectives on how people for whom faith is important negotiate that aspect of their identity amid rapid social and religious change.

Finally, in her quest to integrate the sociology of religion and practical theology, Jackson has an important message for readers beyond the academy. These are the mothers who, like her previous self, have not yet realized that the ground outside the school gate is indeed holy. There is hope for these women within these pages, which must only serve as an encouragement towards the enrichment of their own spiritual lives.

Dr. Gladys Ganiel
Queen's University Belfast

Preface

I have been dropping off and picking up my children at the school gate for fourteen years. My youngest daughter is currently in her penultimate year of primary education and so, when she moves on to secondary school, I will be marking the end of a sixteen year-long chapter of life. Years of loitering in all weathers, in all seasons: feeling awful, feeling on top of the world or feeling just fine, or 'grand,' as we so commonly say in Ireland, when we want to be non-specific and elicit no further query.

The first ten years are a bit of a blur if I'm honest. One daughter was joined by another and then another and mostly the school gate was a logistical nightmare. My chief aim in the day would be to keep a younger child (or two) awake, or asleep, or fed, or entertained as one school run became two, then three at its peak, with a mere forty-five minutes or hour between pick-ups. Life was centered on the car for a number of hours of the day and, as a stay-at-home mum, with only mini-humans for company, I soon realized that some of the time spent parked by the side of the road could provide me with adult interaction.

Some of my friendships emerged as my daughters forged their own fledgling friendships. Ensuing playdates meant trips to other parents' houses, with chats on the doorsteps when I collected them, or a quick cup of tea to mollify children who didn't want to come home yet. Parent social nights gave child-free opportunities for longer chats and some fun; and slowly but surely relationships emerged. Parenting highs and lows, teachers who give too much homework, good plumbers, aging parents, where to source sports equipment and all the essential mundanity of life is shared at the school gate.

As my eldest daughter got older and her strong-willed friends jostled to find their place in the group, I began to realize that the values we were instilling in her at home could have a wider impact on her relations with her classmates. My counsel was often: "Be kind, think about how the other person is feeling when something happens. There must have been a reason for them to lash out like that. Just because someone else is doing it doesn't mean you have to do it too. Look out for the person who seems to find it hard to fit in. Be yourself."

For my part I tried to practice what I preached in my relationships with other mothers. I have tried to be kind, to consciously steer conversations in a positive rather than negative direction, to offer an alternative point of view, to put boundaries in place for my children, to be a listening ear and to work on not being judgmental. All of this is, without doubt, a work in progress. I'm no saint and of course I have been guilty of gossiping at the school gate or staying in my car because I'm feeling anti-social. But my faith, my love for God, is so embedded in me that I can do nothing but see those around me as fellow children of God who, just as I am worthy of God's love, are worthy of my love and care. We are all designed for relationship and wherever we spend the majority of our time; whether it is an office, a hospital ward, a supermarket check-out or in our own homes with our small children; there are myriad opportunities to show God's love in our interactions with those we encounter.

Reflecting on some of the encounters I have had, I clearly remember one at the start of my school gate career. I arrived at my first sports day with a toddler and a baby in a buggy. I was on time, but if I'd been a seasoned parent I'd have known to go early to get a good car parking space in order to reduce my trudging with picnic rug, large bag of snacks, and aforementioned children. After the ignominious performance of my daughter's Yellow Team and it was time to go home, I was struggling with both her existential disappointment and my physical load, when another mum (who I didn't know at all) offered to carry my unwieldy baggage so I could shepherd my tired daughters. She walked out of her way with me to my car. I was hot, bothered, and extremely grateful. She assured me she'd been through it all before me, and remembering the days when children where young and labor intensive, was more than happy to help. This sentiment and generosity really lodged in my heart and mind, and at that point I resolved to be that kind of mum at the school gate. One who took notice, one who offered to help, practically and compassionately, when a need presented itself.

While I chose to stay at home with my daughters (and was fortunate enough financially, to be able to do that), not returning to a workplace outside the home was at times a struggle for me. On dull, dreary days where mundane, repetitive, thankless tasks threatened my sense of self, I questioned if, apart from raising my children, I was contributing anything to society, if my life had any value in the eyes of the world? In all of these instances, and there were many over the years, my husband was my number one cheerleader. As I described my encounters at the school gate and how relationships were developing and deepening in some cases, he encouraged me to begin seeing this as work for God's kingdom: quiet, compassionate, holy work that I was increasingly equipped to do. I was not heading a team of motivated staff to quarterly success or standing at the front of a church preaching a rousing sermon, but by acknowledging the presence of God in everything I do and resting in that gaze of love more consciously, my attitude to the chore of the school gate gradually shifted.

The sacred does not merely belong in church, or during times of private or corporate prayer, or to those dressed in clerical collars and robes. Coming from the Reformed tradition, I have always known this, and yet when taught that so much of the world is sinful, bad and suspect, a sacred/secular divide inevitably crept into my perspective. Barbara Brown Taylor in *An Altar to the World* says:

> Human beings may separate things into as many piles as
> we wish—separating spirit from flesh, sacred from secu-
> lar, church from world. But we should not be surprised
> when God does not recognize the distinctions we make
> between the two. Earth is so thick with divine possibility

that it is a wonder we can walk anywhere without cracking our shins on altars.[1]

There is divine possibility everywhere we inhabit, or as Leah
Abraham posted in shelovesmagazine.com: "The space you take up
is the space you bless."[2] I have been taking up space at the school
gate for almost fifteen years and as those years have gone on, I have
realized I can be a blessing in that important, overlooked, female-
centered location. I can care about people's lives, I can remember that
someone's mother is ill, I can ask how that dreaded family weekend
went, I can offer an attentive, listening ear for the funny, the heart-
breaking, the mundane, and the everyday stuff of life. The school gate
becomes a sacred space by attending to the presence of God there
and being cognizant of the fact that I am a dwelling place for God.

Deciding to return to third level education and study for a
Masters in Applied Spirituality from Waterford Institute of Technology resulted in my dissertation research on School Gate Spirituality. It was a germ of an idea which initially I was hesitant about
voicing, never mind pursuing. It seemed too nebulous, too slight
a topic and yet as I said it out loud to classmates and our research
supervisor, Bernadette Flanagan, it slowly but surely grew wings.
I was pointed in the direction of the field of everyday religion and
found academic affirmation for this notion of God in everyday life.
As I concluded my review of the literature, I wished I could read
wider and further, but deadlines and word counts are cruel masters!
The literature sourced, while providing my research with a strand
of spirituality and religion in which to embed itself, showed that
no one has focused on the school gate as a sacred place, despite its
ubiquity and longevity as a stage in everyday life. I hope my research
question of "Does spirituality make a difference to relationships at
the school gate?" firstly illuminates the school gate, and secondly
confirms it as a special place, a sacred place, and a dynamic place of
encounter where communities continually gather, "cracking shins"
together at the everyday altar of the school gate.

1 Taylor, *Altar in the World*, 15.
2 Abraham, "Immaculate Measure."

Acknowledgments

School gate spirituality is relational and the process of completing this research was also highly relational. Sincere thanks are owed to my academic supervisor Bernadette Flanagan, whose calm, encouragement and belief in this subject gave me confidence in my insights and in my writing. For your invaluable guidance on the methods of research and your steady reassurance I am most grateful.

Thank you to Michael O'Sullivan at the helm of the MA in Applied Spirituality, who along with the other lecturers—Noelia Molina, Brian Dooney, Amanda Dillon, David Halpin, Anne-Marie Dixon, Jack Finnegan, and Niamh Brennan—opened up a view of the vast oceans of spirituality waiting to be explored. My thanks to the staff of the Jesuit Library, Anne, Áine, and June, who all aided my academic efforts by guiding and assisting me in my use of the library.

I want to thank all my wonderful classmates for their part in the story of this year. For your friendship, fun, support, words of comfort and encouragement I am deeply grateful and thankful. Heartfelt gratitude is also due to my spiritual director, Finola, for her accompaniment and support throughout a year which I began immersed in grief for my beloved dad, and emerged with both a Masters and with renewed and expanded faith and wonder.

To my co-researchers and all those who have been part of my story at the school gate, I am deeply grateful for your willingness to share your experiences and for your friendship which means so much to me on a daily basis. We journey on together.

Last, but not least, I want to thank my family for their ongoing support as I studied, especially my aunt Ruth who often held the fort while I went to college. To my husband Damian, I owe huge thanks for being my patient I.T. specialist, my chief encourager, and willing reader of my work. Our daughters Mia, Ruby, and Izzy tell me they too deserve thanks, for without them I would not have spent years at the school gate!

"It is not by great things but by great diligence in little everyday things

that thou canst show great love for God

and become greatly holy and a saint of God.

Few ever do great things and the few who can do them,

can each do but few. . . .

Everyone can by the grace of God be faithful

to what he knows.

Your daily round of duty is your daily path

to come nearer unto God."

Edward Pusey (1800–82)

Introduction

Sandra Schneiders describes Christian spirituality as "the lived experience of Christian faith, which is an ongoing project of life integration in the context of, in response to, and in terms of the revelation of God in Jesus Christ."[3] Spirituality at the school gate is my self-coined phrase to describe how mothers of Christian faith experience, express, and practice their spirituality in the specific, everyday location of their children's school gate. This study will seek to establish whether being intentionally spiritually engaged makes a difference to, and enhances, relationships made in the context of the primary school gate.

This study is located within the porous category of "everyday religion" where sociologists of religion such as Nancy Tatom Ammerman, Robert Orsi, and Meredith McGuire have in the last twenty years, challenged the view that in order to learn about individuals' religious lives one simply looks at affiliation, frequency of attendance, and level of organizational participation. In her book, *Lived Religion: Faith and Practice in Everyday Life*, McGuire clarifies that "religiosity" and "spirituality" are used "more or less interchangeably to refer to how individuals attend to matters of the religious or the spiritual, as they understand those matters at a particular time and context, in their own lives."[4] I would further clarify that in this study "faith" will also be used interchangeably with "spirituality," as a term used more habitually by the co-researchers

---

3. Schneiders, "Biblical Spirituality."
4. McGuire, *Lived Religion*, 6.

who belong to the Protestant tradition, when considering their spiritual life.

I will also be drawing from authors who write from within the field of (accessible) practical theology, and it is therefore noteworthy that Claire E. Wolfteich, while pointing out that practical theology has predominantly been a Protestant discipline, has noted the overlap between the two disciplines:

> Spirituality studies and practical theology share in common a number of features: attention to practices; importance of historical and social context, interdisciplinary methods; concern with cultivating faithful ways of life, interest in appropriation and transformation. At the same time there are marked differences in emphasis, language, and sensibility.[5]

In her discussion of the influence of French historian, philosopher, theologian, and social scientist Michel de Certeau on spirituality studies and practical theology, Wolfteich goes on to acknowledge that while the sociologists of religion mentioned above have "done much to consider spirituality in everyday life . . . quotidian practice is still an area ripe for study, particularly from a theological approach."[6] Philip Sheldrake wrote that "the Christian vocation for de Certeau is increasingly a question of following after the perpetually elusive Christ"[7] and that he believed Christian spirituality could not be settled into a definitive place or establishment. Also taking into account his emphasis on the spiritual quality of everyday practices, de Certeau's perspective mirrors the researcher's and lends weight to this qualitative study of school gate spirituality. Using a heuristic methodology, I will seek to illuminate a previously unresearched element of spirituality in daily life, by interviewing five mothers about the practice of their faith in a specific, everyday social context.

---

5. Wolfteich, "Practices of 'Unsaying,'" 161.

6. Wolfteich, "Practices of 'Unsaying,'" 164.

7. Sheldrake, "Michel de Certeau," 209.

Spirituality Framework

EVERYDAY RELIGION

In this chapter I will set out the spirituality framework from which I approach my exploratory study of spirituality at the school gate. What then is meant by "everyday" or "lived religion" given that it has been established to go beyond the box ticking affiliations, which previously provided the basis for sociological research on religion? In my opinion, lived religion is a blurring of the artificial polarities of sacred and profane, religious and secular, godless and Spirit-filled. In order to explore the dissolving of these dichotomies, Ammerman suggests the following:

> By looking for religion in practice and narratives, we gain a new perspective that allows us to see how spiritual resources are generated, nurtured and deployed across the many religious and secular contexts in which people live their lives.[1]

The school gate as a focus of study is strictly speaking a secular context; but the primary school gates which I and my co-researchers attend are all Protestant, Church of Ireland run schools, with selection processes which prioritize children from parents who are members of Church of Ireland, Presbyterian, Methodist, and Baptist Churches. The so-called sacred/secular divide is thus already hazy, as is the case in the majority of primary education in Ireland. The cultural context for primary schools in the Republic

---

1. Ammerman, *Sacred Stories*, 7.

of Ireland is predominantly linked to religion; with 90 percent of schools run with a Catholic ethos, 5.4 percent a Church of Ireland ethos, and 3.7 percent multi-denominational schools such as Educate Together.[2]

While my focus will be less on the ethos of the *institution* of the school and more on the spiritual practices of the *parents* in their everyday interactions, I acknowledge that researchers such as Ammerman have noted that up until recently:

> Because spirituality is unique to each person, it is treated as sociologically unmeasurable. This methodological dividing line echoes the culture's common wisdom: religion is about institutions that assert external authority, while spirituality is about internal individual pursuits.[3]

I would argue that spirituality, often (but obviously not always), flows from religious institutions and the two should *not* be viewed separately in the way sociologists have done in the past, but rather be regarded as intermingled and vital one to the other. Ammerman saw evidence of this in her research:

> . . . active religious participants are different from those with only loose ties to any religious community, and people in different religious traditions have distinctive patterns for incorporating spirituality in their everyday lives. Organized religion matters, even when the subject is individual spirituality.[4]

This explains the need for bridging terms like everyday and lived religion as they better encompass the individual's internal spirituality and their religion. McGuire believes that, "the term 'lived religion' is useful for distinguishing the actual experience of religious persons from the prescribed religion of institutionally defined beliefs and practices."[5] Robert Orsi argues that "for many people, the world of everyday life is mainly affected by embodied

---

2. Tickner, "Interesting Facts."

3. Ammerman, *Sacred Stories*, 24.

4. Ammerman, *Sacred Stories*, 19.

5. McGuire, *Lived Religion*, 12.

practices, by which the sacred is made vividly real and present through the experiencing body."[6] While the analysis of the data gathered will seek to define the actual experiences and embodied practices of spiritual and religious persons in the context of the school gate, rather than the prescribed doctrines of their religious tradition or school ethos; I think it is important to give the broad religious context out of which such embodied practices flow.

THE REFORMED TRADITION

I was brought up in the Presbyterian tradition, which like the Church of Ireland, is part of the Protestant family of churches. My spirituality therefore stems from the Calvinist tradition, and while I have never read Calvin's work, and have now only encountered it in extract form, I have doubtless absorbed its essences through the teaching in my tradition. As scholars of theology and spirituality have noted the noun "spirituality" was not in common usage in the early Christian tradition and the word itself was foreign to Calvin. Judith Rossall explains that:

> He spoke instead of *pietas* which English translators render as both "piety" and "godliness." The one definition which he gave of *pietas* was brief: "I call piety that reverence joined with love of God, which the knowledge of his benefits induces" (*Institutes* 1.2.1). This piety is an inner disposition which profoundly shapes outer action.[7]

Rossall claims that in his seminal work, *Institutes of the Christian Religion,* Calvin set out to write a spiritual theology, and that: "*pietas* is intimately related to what the believer knows, how she knows it and how that knowledge affects and shapes her way of life; for example, the believer needs to understand the nature of Christ's saving activity in order to find a firm basis for salvation (*Institutes* 2.15.1)."[8] She goes on to say that Calvin's spirituality has

6. McGuire, *Lived Religion*, 13.

7. Rossall, "Reform Spirituality," 140.

8. Rossall, "Reform Spirituality," 141.

to therefore be addressed by means of understanding his theology, rather than just his experience and practices.

The primacy and veracity of the Scriptures to personal faith has always been emphasized in the Protestant tradition and, although I still ascribe huge importance to the Bible, I no longer see every word as being meant to be understood literally and without context. As a child I believed God created the world in seven days: as an adult I now see the creation story as an allegory, and while I still credit God with the role of creator I have discarded the convenient time frame, along with the modern day applicability of much of Leviticus and the right to own slaves. I am however steeped in the stories of Jesus found in the New Testament and this greatly informs my spirituality and the way I live my everyday life. As Rossall says, "the knowledge of God is not simply apprehended rationally; it possesses a Christian, entering deeply into the entire personality. Thus, while doctrine is vital to spirituality it must lead to *transformation* and what is known of God must be worked out in daily living."[9]

When Calvin wrote that, "the useful and life-giving knowledge of God has a specific content. God is known truly when the Christian sees himself as dealing with God in every aspect of his life (*Institutes* 3.7.2, 1.17.2, 3.3.6, 3.3.16 and 3.20.29),"[10] he could not have known that his words would, in the future, provide an excellent definition of everyday spirituality. Philip Sheldrake expands on this when, after charting the journey of spirituality from the patristic period to the contemporary one, he describes Christian spirituality as surveying "the complex mystery of human transformation in the context of a dynamic relationship with God. These days, spirituality seeks to integrate all aspects of human experience and existence."[11]

9. Rossall, "Reform Spirituality," 142.

10. Rossall, "Reform Spirituality," 143.

11. Sheldrake, *Explorations in Spirituality*, 62.

THE INFLUENCE OF THE LONDON INSTITUTE FOR CONTEMPORARY CHRISTIANITY

Moving on from Calvinism to the present-day work of the London Institute for Contemporary Christianity (LICC), part of whose vision statement is: "With Christ, there is no ordinary. With Christ, every encounter, every task, every situation brims with divine possibility,"[12] we see the thread of everyday spirituality spool from the sixteenth to the twenty-first century. This reaches to the heart of my vision of spirituality at the school gate and it has been influenced by LICC and their Executive Director, Mark Greene's book, *Fruitfulness on the Frontline*. "Fruitfulness" is referred to by Jesus when he talks about himself as the true vine, with the disciples as branches who should bear fruit. It also refers to character qualities that the apostle Paul says are the direct result of the work of the Spirit in a believer's life. Greene asks what these fruits of the Spirit, listed by Paul in Galatians 5:22–23 (love, joy, peace, patience, kindness, goodness, faithfulness, gentleness, and self-control),[13] look like where you are? He believes that "fruit is anything done with authentic love" and "anything that brings glory to God."[14] By "frontline" he means "a place or time where we meet fairly regularly with people who don't know Jesus."[15] Greene's framework for fruitfulness on the frontline asks how might you:

1: Model godly character

2: Make good work

3: Minister grace and love

4: Mold culture

5: Be a mouthpiece for truth and justice

6: Be a messenger of the gospel[16]

12. "The London Institute for Contemporary Christianity."

13. All Bible references taken from: *Holy Bible: New International Version*.

14. Greene, *Fruitfulness*, 35.

15. Greene, *Fruitfulness*, 26.

16. Greene, *Fruitfulness*, 38.

During our Sunday church services a few years ago, we watched a series of "Fruitfulness on the Frontline" DVD presentations telling stories of how ordinary people who worked on supermarket checkouts, in offices, and on building sites modeled godly behavior, grace, and love in their everyday lives from Monday to Friday, without necessarily mentioning God or why they were doing it. I realize and acknowledge that what my faith and cultural tradition had embedded in me as the greatest commandment of all, namely: "Love the Lord your God with all your heart and with all your soul and with all your mind . . . and love your neighbor as yourself" (Matthew 22:37–39), is the source of my spirituality at the school gate. What LICC is espousing as a practical way to live out the gospel in everyday life is what I had intuitively and organically been doing at the school gate, due to the self-implicating and transformative nature of my spirituality.

EVERYDAY RELIGION AND THE SCHOOL GATE

In the, albeit narrow, scope of this study I will seek to ascertain if mothers like me from the Protestant faith tradition and with similar theological understanding of how we are to live out the gospel as Christians practice their everyday spirituality at their school gate and whether their relationships with other parents are enhanced by this spirituality. As exemplified by the work of Meredith McGuire and Nancy Ammerman, practices and narratives of everyday spirituality will form the basis of this research from the school gate. In *Lived Religion* McGuire examined four issues to help her understand "real" religion:

> The location of the sacred. Where is the sacred found and how do humans get in touch with it? . . . The nature of divine power. How is divine power exercised in the world? . . . The focus of individual religious expression. How does (or should) the individual integrate religious belief and/or practice with other aspects of life? . . . The

purity and authenticity of religious tradition and group identity. Who is authentically "one of us"?[17]

Having already established that in the Protestant faith tradition from which the co-researchers in this study are situated, the sacred is actively encouraged to merge with the secular and that divine power is not believed to be confined only to God, but resides in all humans through the Holy Spirit; this sacred/secular blurring will to some extent be assumed in the interview questions. I am most interested in McGuire's third question of how the individual integrates their religious belief and practices in other aspects of life, which in this study is the context of the relationships the participants have made at the school gate. Greene's "framework for fruitfulness" will be implicit in the interview questions, as these could be described as techniques for lived faith and spirituality. However, any attempt to "measure" spirituality will be avoided, as the stories of the influence of spirituality on school gate relationships are of most interest in the study.

THE PLACE OF COMPASSION IN THE RESEARCH

Underpinning the framework of everyday spirituality for this study of spirituality at the school gate is the quality of compassion. Before a class which gave us an overview of organic/intuitive inquiry, we were led in a guided meditation focusing on our dissertation topics and encouraged to bring a visual image for our project to mind. To my (Protestant) astonishment an icon of the Sacred Heart of Jesus appeared in my mind and I was in the presence of the wounded, bleeding heart of Jesus. Investigating the topic of the Sacred Heart later, I was drawn to material regarding Blessed Mary of the Divine Heart, to whom, according to a letter dated 23 June 1897, Jesus had made this promise:

> Know this my daughter, that by the charity of my Heart
> I desire to pour out floods of graces through your heart
> over the hearts of others. This is why people will come to

17. McGuire, *Lived Religion*, 21–22.

you with confidence; it will not be your personal qualities which will attract them, but Me. No one, even the
most hardened sinner, will leave your presence without
having received, in one way or another, consolation, re-
lief, or a special grace.[18]

This spoke to me personally in the context of my school gate
spirituality, as I believe that listening to each other is an act of service and compassion and that walking alongside those who are
wounded by life is an act of service and compassion. An authentic self-implicating spirituality must not just be a matter of inner
transformation, for Jesus has instructed us to "Be compassionate
as your Father is compassionate" (Luke 6:36). Sue Monk Kidd says
that, "compassion, which is the very life of God within us, comes
through slow and often difficult metamorphosis deep within the
human soul. It happens through a *process*." She references Meister
Eckhart who believed that, "birthing God essentially meant birthing compassion. He believed compassion to be the ultimate fruit of
our birthing, a slow breaking out of divinity from within us. God is
compassion, he insisted; therefore, as God is born more deeply in
the soul, so too is the compassionate life."[19]

In this study of spirituality at the school gate I know that the
compassion of God, which is mirrored as an ongoing process in
each of us, has informed and motivated how I experience, express,
and practice my spirituality in the everyday environment of a community of parents at a primary school gate. As this is the personal
experience of the researcher, the methodology being employed is a
heuristic one, as according to Bernadette Flanagan:

> Heuristic inquiry is distinctive in that it seeks to pay at-
> tention to the personal character of the data. Heuristic
> inquiry unlike hermeneutics or phenomenology, also
> consciously includes the researcher's own experience
> within the framework of the study. Thus, the researcher

18. *Autobiography of Blessed Mary.*
19. Kidd, *Firstlight.*

has acknowledged the particular features of spiritual experience which she personally finds to be significant.[20]

During this study I will seek to discover if this compassion which I have experienced as both an inflowing from God and outflowing to others, will emerge in the spiritual narratives of my co-researchers at their school gates.

THE IMPORTANCE OF ENCOUNTER

While compassion underpins the researcher's spiritual experience, the school gate provides the opportunity and location for repeated encounters where compassion can emerge. Encounter is central to Jesus in his earthly ministry. Rather than teaching in the synagogue, Jesus was an itinerant preacher and often taught his disciples more about the kingdom of God through his interactions with those he met on his journeys, than by his sermons. Luke 8:40–56 shows us that Jesus' attentiveness to suffering meant that, despite being crushed by a crowd on his way to go and heal Jairus' daughter, he was instantly aware when the woman who had been bleeding for twelve years touched his cloak and was healed by her faith. He stopped and asked "Who touched me?" (v. 45) and when the hitherto outcast woman reluctantly identified herself, he extended her physical healing to a cultural and emotional healing by calling her "daughter," which Ruth Patterson in *The Gaze of Love* describes as affirming her as a daughter of Abraham who is fully acceptable to the community.[21]

Jesus, as God's son, was able to discern and meet the woman's complex physical, psychological, and emotional needs in a single encounter. In our earthly encounters we need relationships to grow and strengthen before we can emulate this attentiveness, compassion, and practical care, but I suggest that this is exactly the opportunity that the daily, repetitive nature of the school gate presents.

20. Flanagan, "Liberty God."
21. Patterson, *The Gaze of Love*, 126.

In *The Tenderness of God* Gillian T. W. Ahlgren looks at the lives of Francis and Clare of Assisi and shows through their lives and ministries that "we can learn love, from God, and from one another, as we share life together in graced encounter."[22] Encounter is, simply put, a meeting or an interaction between people; but Ahlgren believes that, "When done in the conscious presence of the love of God, encounter creates sacred space in the human community. Encounter moves us from observers of life to collaborators with God, in the building up of the human community, the creation of a common home."[23] This research seeks to discover if the school gate community can be a sacred place, if those who acknowledge the dwelling of God within them see encounter in their everyday lives at the school gate as potentially sacred.

CONCLUSION

In summary the spiritual framework for this study primarily follows the work of Nancy Ammerman and Meredith McGuire and is couched within the theory of everyday or lived spirituality. Ahlgren says, "We participate in the making of places sacred as we attend to the presence of God that already dwells there and as we open ourselves to be vessels of that presence in our world."[24] This study will look at spiritual experiences, expressions, and practices of mothers within their context of an Irish, Protestant school gate, where the sacred and secular may prove to be indistinct, due to the cultural and religious backgrounds of the participants involved.

22. Ahlgren, *Tenderness of God*, xiii.
23. Ahlgren, *Tenderness of God*, 36.
24. Ahlgren, *Tenderness of God*, 112.

Literature Review

INTRODUCTION

In this study I intend "school gate spirituality" as a metaphor for how individual women bring their spirituality to the community formed at the school gate. It will be considered from within the context of everyday religion, which began emerging from the school of sociology of religion in the 1990s. As a phenomenon it gained prominence in the early twentieth century, due to the collective work of Nancy Ammerman, Robert Orsi, and Meredith McGuire, who have developed a new way of understanding what spirituality is and how it manifests itself in a society. Instead of focusing on affiliations to, and practices defined by religious institutions, they "draw attention to the lived expression of a spirituality in people's everyday lives."[1] Here I will mainly refer to the work of Ammerman and McGuire as they tackle the subject in a wide ranging way, using a phenomenological approach, which was hugely informative to my background research. Orsi's case studies are ethnographic and focus on individuals' stories in order to illuminate their everyday religion and proved to be less transferable to this study.

Despite the impressive range of data associated with everyday religion which has been reviewed by Ammerman and McGuire, there is a North American focus to their work, and while the cultural contexts of the U.S. and Ireland have many similarities, there are obviously also differences which require an approach specific

1. Flanagan and O'Sullivan, "Spirituality in Contemporary Ireland," 55–73.

to the Irish cultural context. I will refer to the work of Bernadette Flanagan for a European/Irish perspective on the specific spirituality of women and also Claire E. Wolfteich, another U.S. scholar who has written on how women's spirituality and mothering impacts on their role in public leadership, rather than in the more commonplace, quotidian realm of the school gate. In the realm of popular, practical theology and spirituality writing, I have considered a number of reflection-informed practice books, all of which use an overarching metaphor to describe their lived example of spirituality in a community context.

EVERYDAY RELIGION

Ammerman's most recent book *Sacred Stories Spiritual Tribes: Finding Religion in Everyday Life* has proved invaluable. Her premise is that "all institutional boundaries—including religious ones—are porous"[2] and asks if all the ways that "faith finds its way into a life count as religion, what does it look like in the workplace or in the home?"[3] By opening up the definitions and boundaries of what constitutes religion, Ammerman seeks to explore religion across a fuller spectrum than sociologists of religion have done previously, by paying attention to "practices and narratives more than tightly argued philosophical systems."[4] She highlights narratives as something sociologists and psychologists have increasingly realized that humans use to give order to their world and claims that, "stories are important, in part, because they are not merely personal. They exist at the intersection of personal and public."[5]

This intersection is for me the pivot point of everyday religion, where an individual's spirituality manifests itself in their public sphere and in the case of this study, at the school gate. Ammerman also wanted to identify what kinds of situations in everyday life call

2. Ammerman, *Sacred Stories*, 6.
3. Ammerman, *Sacred Stories*, 7.
4. Ammerman, *Sacred Stories*.
5. Ammerman, *Sacred Stories*, 8.

forth spiritual accounts, and who listens to these sacred tales from the people she calls "spiritual tribes." In her study she recognized the impossibility of studying all the stories everyone tells about everyday life, and using ninety-five participants from two cities, Boston and Atlanta, looked at what activities might cultivate and concentrate attention on the spiritual dimension of life. Key to her findings was that, "what people name as definitional to their religious identity is rarely a doctrine or even a spiritual experience. What they name is a way of living."[6]

Meredith McGuire is also a sociologist of religion, and like Ammerman argues that when examining religious lives it is more productive to look at individuals and their experiences and practices, rather than creating mountains of qualitative sociological data focused on affiliation and organizational participation. In *Lived Religion* she states: "The focus throughout this book is on how religion and spirituality are practiced, experienced, and expressed by ordinary people (rather than official spokespersons) in the context of their everyday lives."[7]

She seeks to address how "embodied practices can effectively link the material aspects of people's lives with the spiritual"[8] and by examining lived religion seeks to get closer to understanding the complexity and diversity of individual religion. While Ammerman's initial mapping of her data yielded what she calls "cultural packages," she grouped them in the following manner before examining:

1. Theistic

2. Extra-Theistic

3. Ethical spirituality of moral goodness

4. Spiritual but not religious[9]

---

6. Ammerman, *Sacred Stories*, 214.
7. McGuire, *Lived Religion*, 12.
8. McGuire, *Lived Religion*, 13.
9. Ammerman, *Sacred Stories*, 25.

McGuire does not pre-categorize her study participants and instead specifically looks at two different cultural groups: U.S. Latinos and Latinas as examples of popular religious expressions today, and then at southern white evangelicals as a popular religion in practice today.

MEASURES OF SPIRITUALITY

In a co-authored paper "Linking Religion and Spirituality with Psychological Well-Being: Examining Self-actualization, Meaning in Life, and Personal Growth Initiative," Ivtzan et al. "delineate the two constructs and categorize participants into different groups based on measured levels of religious involvement and spirituality."[10] The four groups were:

1. High level of religious involvement and spirituality

2. A low level of religious involvement with a high level of spirituality

3. A high level of religious involvement with a low level of spirituality

4. A low level of religious involvement and spirituality[11]

After scoring the groups against specific measures of psychological well-being (self-actualization, meaning in life, and personal growth initiative), the importance of spirituality on psychological well-being was confirmed, regardless of whether it is experienced through religious participation. A sample of 205 was used and a complex variety of scales used (Spiritual Transcendence Scale, Short Index of Self-Actualization, Meaning in Life Questionnaire, and Personal Growth Initiative), to reach the result. This quantitative method contrasts with the qualitative, ethnographic, or phenomenological approaches employed by McGuire and Ammerman, who wanted to move beyond quantitative examinations; which Ammerman believes, even when they took both religion and

10. Ivtzan et al., "Linking Religion and Spirituality," 915.

11. Ivtzan et al., "Linking Religion and Spirituality."

spirituality into account, cannot measure the "implicitly individual and interior nature of spirituality."[12] For this Ammerman argues you need to carry out interviews that "look for the way definitions [of spirituality] show up in conversations about everyday life."[13]

EVANGELICALISM

While McGuire's findings on U.S. evangelicals do provide a backdrop for this study, they cannot shine a full beam of light on the particular context of Irish evangelical Protestantism. However, when she acknowledges that the extent of terminology attributed to Protestant religiosity, "e.g., 'mainline', 'fundamentalist', 'pentecostal', 'liberal', and 'conservative' are not easy to apply to individuals simply on the basis of their religious affiliation,"[14] I would concur with this uneasiness in labeling individuals within the tradition. Furthermore, I would suggest that the participants in this study would prefer the term "Christian" (one who follows Christ), who happens to attend a Presbyterian church; rather than even the term evangelical, which has become increasingly negatively loaded with the terms McGuire mentions above.

It is worth clarifying at this point what is actually meant by evangelical, and I refer here to the work of Gladys Ganiel who describes evangelicalism in Ireland as having:

> Its origins in eighteenth-century revival movements in English Anglicanism and continental pietism. Evangelical history in Ireland is generally dated from 1747, when Wesley made his first visit to the island. Evangelicalism then, as now, was a diverse movement, encompassing Christians in a variety of denominations. Bebbington's (1989) four-fold definition of evangelicalism rings true for those original revivalists and those who would be considered evangelicals today. The characteristics that he identifies are that evangelicals believe that one must be

12. Ammerman, *Sacred Stories*, 24.

13. Ammerman, *Sacred Stories*.

14. McGuire, *Lived Religion*, 71.

converted or "born again"; that the Bible is the inspired word of God; that Christ's death on the cross was a historical event necessary for salvation; and that Christians must express their faith through social action/evangelism.[15]

Acknowledging the importance of Scripture to evangelicals, but stating that specific beliefs are less important for the purposes of understanding their lived religion than their Bible-focused *practices,* McGuire believes that the experiential aspect which characterizes evangelicals creates an "expectation of certain specific kinds of ongoing experiences of the divine in one's own life."[16]

COMMUNITY: PRACTICAL THEOLOGY AND REFLECTION-BASED PRACTICE

This ongoing expectation of the active presence of the divine in our lives, is the common thread in the "non-academic" books I have read. As school gate spirituality is the practice of spirituality in a specific community setting, I gathered books which each use a different metaphor for lived spirituality in action in a specific context. I regularly listen to a series of podcasts hosted by Jen Hatmaker from Austin, Texas, who is a Christian author and public speaker with an influential social media presence. She has a podcast called "For the Love of . . ." and runs series on topics such as People, Home, Stories, Family, Jesus, Community, Food, and Culture.[17] It was during a series on "For the Love of Community" that I heard Kristin Schell talk to Hatmaker about her "ministry of presence" in the local community and her subsequent book *The Turquoise Table*[18] which describes her experience.

Schell was on the one hand inspired by Romans 12:13: "Take every opportunity to open your life and home to others," and on the other hand frustrated by the busyness of family life and endless

15. Ganiel, *Evangelicalism and Conflict*, 3.

16. McGuire, *Lived Religion*, 72.

17. "Jen Hatmaker."

18. Schell, *Turquoise Table*.

extra-curricular activities. She heard a story at a Christian conference about Ludmilla, an eighty-four-year-old widow in Prague who simply opens her home every day to friends and strangers who need to talk. Inspired by Ludmilla, and recognizing the dearth of community where texting instead of talking is the norm, Schell realized that she didn't know her neighbors. So, she bought a basic picnic table at the hardware store, painted it turquoise to make it stand out, and plonked it in her front yard. The "Turquoise Table" was born. She would regularly sit out at the table for a period of time and began by firstly noticing what was going on in her neighborhood, before slowly beginning to build relationships. Comparing the turquoise table to the old village well where women would meet daily for water and conversation she says: "I can imagine women sharing similar struggles and stories around the village well hundreds of years ago. It's what women do. We're drawn to each other and our stories and through that experience oneness. It's how community is built: layer by layer, struggle by struggle, story by story."[19]

While Schell is a Christian and sees her ministry of presence as emanating from her understanding of her Christian faith, she does not use her table to proselytize to her community. Instead she simply recognizes that as people we are wounded and that "we need people—free of judgment, but full of wisdom—and time. Healing happens in community with other people."[20] Dale and Jonalyn Fincher, who co-authored *Coffee Shop Conversations: Making the Most of Spiritual Small Talk*,[21] also favor creating an atmosphere conducive to spiritual conversations, but with the added layer of intentional evangelism playing in the background. As they describe conversations with friends and acquaintances in their lives, they are influenced by their understanding of Jesus telling us to love your neighbor as yourself as being, "he means to love your neighbor because that is who *you* are. Our humanity inescapably connects us to our neighbor."[22]

19. Schell, *Turquoise Table*, 77.
20. Schell, *Turquoise Table*, 141–42.
21. Fincher and Fincher, *Coffee Shop Conversations*.
22. Fincher and Fincher, *Coffee Shop Conversations*, 217.

"LOVE THE LORD YOUR GOD WITH ALL YOUR HEART AND LOVE YOUR NEIGHBOR AS YOURSELF"

As Jesus himself termed this the greatest commandment of all, it is no surprise that it functions as an instigator and a common thread in reflection-based practice books which examine spirituality in everyday life. Laura Everett, in *Holy Spokes: The Search for Urban Spirituality*,[23] uses the daily, intentional practice of commuter cycling as a metaphor for her urban spirituality and says, "that whole 'love thy neighbor' thing is a lot easier to do when you actually *see* your neighbors."[24] Cycling in the city of Boston opened up a whole side of the city that had been hidden from her while commuting by car. Like Schell she recognized that the habits of our daily lives can make the "anonymous become particular"[25] and a love and concern for our neighbor results in better communities. The communal sharing of pain is described not in the context of the table, but in the metaphor of the cyclist's journey: "We ride further when we ride together. When I go out on my own, I can ride far, but I can go further with someone else. Companions don't eliminate my experience of pain, but they help me realize I'm not experiencing it alone."[26]

As well as using the metaphor of all the different bicycle components, that together form a functioning mode of transport, which she compares to different aspects of her spirituality, Everett also draws upon the inspirational life of Brother Lawrence who joined a Carmelite monastery in Paris in the 1600s. He had no education and never became a priest, spending most of his time working in the monastery kitchen, and yet, "his writing would be collected and become the book *The Practice of the Presence of God,* one of the most revered works of spirituality about cultivating mindfulness in the everyday."[27] For Everett "cycling is a solitary

23. Everett, *Holy Spokes*.
24. Everett, *Holy Spokes*, 3.
25. Everett, *Holy Spokes*, 27.
26. Everett, *Holy Spokes*, 39.
27. Everett, *Holy Spokes*, 7.

activity done in community,"[28] and spirituality is a personal relationship with God worked out in community with those around
us: love God, love your neighbor.

Schell wanted to "make a place where we all feel comfortable
and safe"[29] at her turquoise table and in this study I will seek to
discover if is this achievable at the school gate when spirituality
is brought there? Or, to push this idea further, can an individual's
spirituality enable *them* to be an embodied place where others feel
comfortable and safe? This embodied spirituality was evident in
the life of Everett's spiritual inspiration Brother Lawrence, who
lived with the core conviction that all the things we do can be done
in ways that draw us closer to God.

WOMEN AND THE SCHOOL GATE

While the extensive studies of Ammerman and McGuire looked at
everyday religion in both the workplace and the family home, the
school gate was overlooked as a noteworthy setting. Addressing
the fact that gender profoundly affects people's lived religion, Mc-
Guire highlighted the preparation of food by women and eating
as an example of embodied practices which have spiritual meaning but are overlooked by many religious traditions. She argues
that boundaries between sacred and profane which were created
during the Long Reformation "effectively marginalized much of
women's religious contribution, especially their domestic religious
practices."[30] She recommends that:

> In order to understand women's lived religion fully, we
> need to appreciate their ritual practices centered on the
> so called private, domestic, familial sphere, where their
> roles are likely to be more active and expressive. These
> private sphere rituals are at least as important as par-
> ticipation in the public, organizational sphere, where

28. Everett, *Holy Spokes*, 116.
29. Schell, *Turquoise Table*, 124.
30. McGuire, *Lived Religion*, 106.

women's ritual roles have traditionally been more passive or non-existent.[31]

Like the home, the school gate is a place where women predominate, and I would suggest that it is an extension of the familial sphere, with women being chiefly responsible for the culture created there. Given that it functions as a significant part of parents' lives for at least fourteen years, it is therefore worth noting as a site of cultural and sociological import. In addition, for those mothers who do not work outside of the home for at least some of that period, their involvement at the school gate could almost be described as constituting a part-time job, as schools seek more and more parental involvement from an ever dwindling pool of "non-working" parents. For those mothers who have an active, lived spirituality, the community at the school gate is an obvious place in which to express this spirituality.

WOMEN'S LIFE WRITING

Claire Wolfteich poses the following questions in her essay: "Spirituality, Mothering, and Public Leadership: Women's Life Writing and Generative Directions for Spirituality Studies":

> How do we, as scholars of Christian spirituality, retrieve, adapt, name, and/or construct a fund of spiritual vocabulary, imagery, and practice rich enough, resonant enough, moving enough, to speak to and give voice to contemporary people? More specifically . . . I wonder: where do mothers find ourselves, those of us whose spiritual landscapes are not deserts or convents, our primary practices not often including pilgrimages or retreats?[32]

Acknowledging that we know very little about the "concrete, everyday practices of mothering as experienced not by celibate elders but by laywomen embedded in the day-to-day care of

---

31. McGuire, *Lived Religion*, 108.

32. Wolfteich, "Spirituality, Mothering, and Public Leadership," 145.

children,"[33] she suggests that life writing is a significant source which "could be used more widely by spirituality scholars in addressing the lacunae in scholarship on mothering and spirituality."[34] She goes on to look at three case studies in Spirituality (Dorothy Day, Dolores Huerta, and Lena Frances Edwards), with attention focused on mothering, work, and public leadership. While one of her aims in this article (and in her subsequent book) is to articulate more fully the complexity of mothering as a dimension of Christian spirituality; her focus is more on the interplay between vocational and spiritual narratives, rather than on the spiritual experiences of someone engaged in "full-time" mothering—a contentious and inadequate phrase—whose "frontline"[35] is the school gate, rather than a public leadership role.

Bernadette Flanagan in her chapter on "Women and Spirituality" in *The Bloomsbury Guide to Spirituality* also examines women's spiritual autobiographies as a distinctive example of what she calls the global turn to spirituality, recognizing the fact that there is a "demand for narratives that tell stories of authentic spiritual seeking in manifold forms."[36] Flanagan goes on to look at the writings of Elizabeth Gilbert, Tenzin Palmo, and Elaine MacInnes who were all on spiritual journeys broadly within the Buddhist tradition, and Kathleen Norris who writes from a Christian perspective. Themes such as the female spiritual quest or pilgrimage, the need for female spiritual teachers or mystics, and the body as a source of spiritual awakening are all drawn upon by these writers. Flanagan concludes that these spiritual narratives are "resources of empowerment and guidance for present and future generations of women."[37] While in agreement with this, I would also concur with Wolfteich, who suggests that as the field of autobiography studies expands, spirituality scholars will have a route "to study

---

33. Wolfteich, "Spirituality, Mothering, and Public Leadership," 146.

34. Wolfteich, "Spirituality, Mothering, and Public Leadership," 147.

35. Greene, *Fruitfulness*.

36. Flanagan, "Women and Spirituality," 329.

37. Flanagan, "Women and Spirituality," 335.

non-elites."[38] It is precisely a sample of these non-elites, who have not published or, indeed, even considered writing their spiritual autobiographies, that I will interview. In doing so, I hope to construct a view of their somewhat hidden and undervalued spiritual lives, within the context of their highly contextualized and culturally specific school gate community.

CONCLUSION

In conclusion, while there is an excellent range of qualitative research available in the field of lived or everyday religion, which has been invaluable to my aim of locating the topic of school gate spirituality within this framework; I have not discovered an academic writer who has focused on this specific context of the school gate in any of the North American or European cultural settings examined. Taking into account the cultural and religious context of this research study means that the brief discussion of Irish evangelicalism does inform the Irish Protestant context of the women involved. In the example of quantitative research examined, while a strong link was established between spirituality and psychological well-being, which is useful, the sociological scales employed were recognized as unemployable in this study and ultimately too limited in their outcomes.

In the field of popular, practice-based reflection books, I discovered many examples of using a metaphor drawn from everyday life to inform and discuss spirituality on both an individual and community level; but none that specifically included the school gate. Finally, examining a number of women's spirituality life writing is an encouraging signpost to the fact that the academy is beginning to realize that women's spiritual insights, wisdom, and indeed questions are important and have yet to be mined sufficiently. In this study I hope to add to the body of spiritual insights from mothers who practice a dynamic, lived spirituality in their daily lives at the school gate.

38. Wolfteich, "Spirituality, Mothering, and Public Leadership," 147.

Methodology

INTRODUCTION

According to Kees Waaijman, research should revolve around two questions: what are the fundamental *characteristics* which define the area of reality to be studied; and what *methodology* is best suited to this area of reality?[1] I would assert that while the characteristics of spirituality at the school gate are specific, in that a school gate community and members of that community who display an active spirituality define the parameters of the study; this is however an area of spiritual interplay which has not yet been investigated, and the research is therefore exploratory within the established field of lived or everyday religion. The methodology employed in this inquiry of school gate spirituality is heuristics.

HEURISTICS: A DESCRIPTION

Defining heuristics, Clark Moustakas explains that the root meaning of heuristic comes from the Greek word *heuriskein*, meaning to discover or to find, and that:

> It refers to a process of internal search through which one discovers the nature and meaning of experience and develops methods and procedures for further investigation and analysis. The self of the researcher is present

---

1. Waaijman, *Forms, Foundations, Methods*, 307.

throughout the process . . . and also experiences growing
self-awareness and self-knowledge.[2]

As primary researcher it was my own experiences of spirituality at the school gate that led to the research question under
discussion. According to Moustakas there are six phases of heuristic research:

1. Initial engagement: when the personal experience of the researcher leads to the choice of a particular topic

2. Immersion: the researcher becomes absorbed in the topic
   and expectant of finding meaning with regard to it in all areas
   of their life

3. Incubation: the researcher retreats from the intense, concen-
   trated focus on the question and allows the subconscious to
   continue to grow the scope of the topic

4. Illumination: the researcher's receptivity creates new insights,
   clarifies, confirms, or corrects meanings

5. Explication: using focusing, indwelling, self-searching, and
   self-disclosure the purpose of this phase is to fully examine
   what has awakened in consciousness

6. Culmination of the research in a creative synthesis: once fa-
   miliar with all the data in its major constituents, qualities,
   and themes, a narrative depiction is created paying heed to
   tacit, intuitive, and self-searching powers.[3]

VALIDATION OF HEURISTIC RESEARCH

As heuristic inquiry uses qualitative methodological approaches
to arrive at themes and narratives of experience, validity is *not* a
quantitative measurement determined by correlations or statistics.
Rather the question of validity is one of meaning, and this judgment is made by the primary researcher. In order to ensure a valid

2. Moustakas, *Heuristic Research*, 9.

3. Moustakas, *Heuristic Research*, 27–33.

depiction of the experience being investigated, Moustakas recommends enhancing verification through triangulation, by both returning repeatedly to the data and then returning to the research participants to check if the researcher's interpretation of their contribution is what they intended to convey. In this study each participant was sent a transcription of their interview and invited to check its veracity. During the process of thematic content analysis, the data was repeatedly referred to over a number of weeks.

SELECTION OF RESEARCH PARTICIPANTS

In selecting potential interviewees, or co-researchers as they are referred to in heuristic inquiry, I adopted purposive sampling to increase the validity of my findings. In this approach one chooses a particular subject group because it illustrates some feature or process in which the researcher is interested.[4] In my case I was interested in whether mothers with a vibrant spirituality feel that this has an impact on their relationships at the school gate. It was vital therefore that my participants exhibited this spirituality, so a convenient sample was also used, as before undertaking interviews I could personally verify the presence of their spirituality in their church context. Initial contact was made by personal encounter as the participants are all known to the researcher.

AN OVERVIEW OF THE PARTICIPANTS

The profile of the participants was as follows: five married females aged between 40–49 with one, two, two, three, and three children respectively. They all were born into the Protestant tradition and currently attend a Presbyterian church in Dublin and their children are, or have been, pupils at Church of Ireland national schools in south Dublin. In addition, they would all refer to themselves as Christians, who attempt to integrate their faith into their everyday lives and therefore fitted the inclusion criteria of the study.

4. Silverman, *Doing Qualitative Research*, 141, 281.

ETHICS

Ethical approval on behalf of Waterford Institute of Technology was sought and obtained before embarking on the project. Consent by the co-researchers to their participation in the study was initially given verbally and prior to their interview they received a "Letter inviting participation in the Research Project," a "Participant Information Leaflet," and a "Consent Form" to sign and return. All four co-researchers were assured about the confidentiality and anonymity of their interview responses. In order to safeguard their anonymity, pseudonyms have been used for both them, their children, and the names of their schools. As primary researcher these safeguarding criteria have also been applied to my contributions to the data. It is noteworthy that granting anonymity counters "question threat," which is a term used by William Foddy to denote the risk that interviewees' responses to questions do not reflect their actual opinions but are tailored to what they perceive to be acceptable in the social context of the interview.[5]

DATA COLLECTION PROCESS: THE INTERVIEWS

There are many definitions of interviews but Kumar says, "any person-to-person interaction, either face to face or otherwise, between two or more individuals with a specific purpose in mind is called an interview."[6] As stated previously the intention of the interviews was to explore the participants' experience of their spirituality in the realm of their relationships with other parents at the school gate. The best way to access this sort of information is through in-depth, semi-structured interviews. This method is preferable to surveys or questionnaires, which provide less scope for deep or follow-up questioning. Prior to the interviews, at the time of consenting to participate in the research project, the co-researchers were verbally told that there would be four areas of discussion: personal information, information about your school,

5. Foddy, *Constructing Questions*, 121.
6. Kumar, *Research Methodology*, 144.

a description of your personal faith, and your experience of spirituality at the school gate. They were not provided with a full set of questions as I didn't want them to feel they had to create answers, if in fact the question did not resonate with their experience. Due to the discursive nature of the interviews, questions were not always asked in the same order, nor phrased in exactly the same way. However, in each interview I attempted to cover the same subject matter, using the pre-formulated question sheet.[7]

It is acknowledged that a higher level of interviewing skills is required in a semi-structured as opposed to a structured interview and that in certain situations it is possible for an investigator to obtain further information by verbally probing and also by observation of non-verbal reactions in the participants. A small introductory amount of straightforward, closed questions were initially asked to elicit factual information and to set the co-researchers at ease, and for the main part of the interviews open-ended questions were used to seek opinions, perceptions, and attitudes on the topic. In the forming of these questions I took note of Ammerman, who in *Sacred Stories, Spiritual Tribes* advised that, "by consistently framing questions in ways that asked about actions and events and decisions, people fell easily into telling stories rather than providing checklist answers."[8]

DATA ANALYSIS

While open-ended questions provide a wealth of in-depth information, a process of content analysis is required to classify the data. The interviews were recorded and listened to in their entirety by the primary researcher before being transcribed. As previously stated, in the six-stage process required in heuristic inquiry, content analysis includes incubation, illumination, and explication which culminates in a creative synthesis of the insights gathered through reflection. As Bernadette Flanagan points out, "recording

7. See Appendix.
8. Ammerman, *Sacred Stories*, 14.

research findings in spirituality requires listening for the still small voice of Spirit within the spoken words, actions and interactions of the informant."[9] This quieting of the Spirit in the researcher aided in the process of illumination before data analysis began and enabled the insights to emerge over a period of time, as did returning to the data and checking the veracity of the transcript content with the co-researchers.

Thematic content analysis was used to organize and structure the accumulated interview data following the six-stage process of coding identified by Newell and Burnard in *Research for Evidence-Based Practice in Healthcare*.[10] Extensive general notes were firstly identified from the five transcripts before undertaking a process of "open coding" to summarize these notes into initial categories. Where these categories overlapped, they were then "collapsed" into what emerged as eight final themes. The data was color-coded to correspond to a theme and then cut and pasted under these themed headings, before being presented in the "Findings" chapter.

LIMITATIONS

The limitations of the study are primarily in its scope: the sample size was small and drawn from only one Christian tradition. Many schools in Ireland, especially in larger towns and cities, are now strongly multi-cultural and an analysis of spirituality in this context would provide a broader picture. The study was based solely in middle-class Dublin and it is acknowledged that including rural settings would also garner more diverse experiences. The analysis, while rich in content is therefore specific and not representative of all school gate spirituality. The study should be viewed as a starting point for a wider treatment of the topic, as it provides insightful evidence of the impact spirituality at the school gate can have on relationships, and shines a light on a much under-researched section of the population, namely mothers and their experiences.

9. Flanagan, "Quaestio Divina," 135.

10. Newell and Burnard, *Research for Evidence-Based Practice*, 121–29.

CONCLUSION

This study of spirituality at the school gate is an exploratory one, couched within the field of everyday religion and employs heuristic methodology. The co-researchers were a purposive, convenient sample and interviewed using a semi-structured method. The data analysis yielded rich, but limited results, which suggests further research would be of benefit to the academy of spirituality studies.

Findings

INTRODUCTION

In this section I will present the data from the interviews conducted with five mothers whose child or children currently attend national school and one who was there for eleven years up until last year. They are all Protestants, who attend a Presbyterian church, and are educated to third level, with four of them professionally qualified. While only two originate from Dublin, all have lived in south Dublin for over fifteen years, are married, and live in middle-class areas. One co-researcher works from home on a part-time basis, two are stay-at-home parents, and two work part-time outside of the home. The following sections will examine eight key themes that emerged from the data.

SCHOOL GATE DYNAMICS

All the co-researchers have children who attend Church of Ireland national schools in south Dublin and have spent many cumulative years at their respective school gates. While three parents live close enough to walk, bike, or scoot to school with their children, a car will often be used especially at the end of the school day, if after-school activities necessitate an onward journey. At pick-up, parents either enter the school property or wait outside a gate with other parents for their children to return to them. One mother now allows her daughter to walk home with a friend, and is therefore now infrequently at the school gate. The gate is the main point of contact between parents and the arena where relationships can be made. Other opportunities, which all co-researchers availed of with varying regularity throughout the school year, include nights out for mums (and dads) or coffee mornings organized by class reps. It was remarked that one class group of parents may be more sociable than others; somewhat predictably this commitment to sociability usually coincided with the first year of entry into the school system.

In addition to organized social nights one co-researcher talked about walking or running with other parents after the morning drop-off and building up strong relationships in this manner. Where parks and coffee shops are nearby, and parents have time to fill between two pick-ups, then ad hoc socializing with children occurs. As children get older and only one pick-up is required this contact reduces and may almost disappear altogether if the child can walk home independently. While many working parents are able to drop off their own children, only those who work part-time in the mornings can pick up and as a result there are also a number of childminders or grandparents in attendance, which all co-researchers agreed diminished the chances to get to know the parents:

> . . . the norm is if you don't see the parents at the school gate and have that frequent interaction you have less of a bond and you just don't know them that well. There were at least two children where I think I've met the parents once or twice the whole time. . . . Because they were working full-time they were not able to attend sports days and things like that.[1]

A number of comments were made about how children who are looked after by childminders or afterschool services lose out socially as they tend not to be invited on playdates or be able to spontaneously go to the park after school.

While all the schools are Church of Ireland and due to admissions policies at least one parent will have links to a Protestant church, there are many Protestant/Catholic marriages and so

1. C, "Interview."

friendships that are formed are not necessarily along religious lines. All co-researchers had friends with "no discernible faith" and one child had ascertained that she was the only one in her class who attends church on a weekly basis. While occasional politics and bitchiness were mentioned in passing by two co-researchers, most school gates were classed as very friendly, caring, and sociable.

A school gate with the area where parents congregate before collecting children. Photo credit: Diane Jackson

TIME

The passage of time and its effect on the school gate experience was mentioned by two co-researchers. One, who has one daughter, sees a big difference from the early years: " . . . definitely since the beginning there seemed to be people around more than they are now. I think there are quite a lot of people that have retrained and gone back to work full-time."[2]

2. A, "Interview."

In terms of arranging social events, time pressure for families was therefore noted. "I just always feel that people are too busy now. . . . So when you try to think about when you could possibly meet there really aren't very many times."[3] While after school activities such as hockey or swimming engendered spending an hour with other parents and allowed for longer, more in-depth chats the brevity of time involved in drop off and collection was noted by one co-researcher who said, "you wouldn't have much time really . . . a lot of people are in their cars or only come at the last moment. You don't really get much time to talk . . . and then if you're in a group of people rather than one to one it's difficult as well."[4] By contrast one co-researcher who was not rushing from work arrived early most days in order to get a park and would have an extra ten minutes which she used to chat, either one to one in a car or at the gate with a small group.

LINKS BETWEEN THE LOCAL PARISH CHURCH AND SCHOOL

All co-researchers agreed that the church attached to the patronage of their school had a positive influence on the ethos of their school, with all the schools inviting the Rector or Curate to take either weekly or monthly assemblies, and all the school children being invited to family services at Christmas and Easter. At least one school holds an end-of-year service in the church with full participation by the pupils. Confirmation classes for sixth class Anglican pupils was another link, though one co-researcher noted that there was less enthusiasm in her school for children of Catholic background leaving the building to attend First Communion classes in the local Catholic Church. It was also suggested that the parish could do more to foster links between the church and school instead of just expecting parents to help out at events such as fetes. A number of parishes distribute their monthly newsletter

3. A, "Interview."
4. D, "Interview."

to the parents as part of the school newsletter, which means information is disseminated about activities relevant to children such as Brownies, Guides, Cub Scouts, and Sunday School.

The co-researchers remarked that the influence of a head or class teacher effected the ethos of a school and how religion as a subject was taught or prioritized, with the teachers who had a committed faith being more enthusiastic in religion lessons. One child remarked to her mother that she could tell if the teacher believed in God or not by how they taught religion. In a school where it appears no faith is discernible in the headteacher, a lack of compassion in a number of situations has been noted by one co-researcher, while the opposite is true in a school where it seems like faith is important to the headteacher.

PERSONAL FAITH AND SOURCES OF SPIRITUALITY

All co-researchers regularly attend a Presbyterian church on Sundays which, while it forms the backdrop of their faith and provides a core community, is by no means the only source of their spirituality. All co-researchers talked about the importance of small groups who either study the Bible or read a spiritual book together. One co-researcher is a member of a group with a very diverse age and background range. They explore the Bible passage which was used as the basis of the previous Sunday's sermon asking, "How does this work out in real life? How do I take this from head knowledge to real life?"[5] When members come and go it can play havoc with the group dynamic and levels of trust, but when deep relationships form they promote "more honesty, more vulnerability and more accountability."[6] All co-researchers reference the importance of relationships in the sustaining of their faith, both with God and other people, with support from small groups being mentioned by everyone as being places:

5. A, "Interview."
6. A, "Interview."

where we can share struggles and inspire and encourage each other, share the books we're reading, run thoughts past each other, so I would say it's very important for my faith in terms of being an encouragement and support. And then in the background knowing that we're praying for each other during the week.[7]

This was especially crucial to the co-researcher, who along with her husband, was not born in Ireland and therefore has no family members living here. By necessity she can only rely on friends for support on a day to day basis.

While regular attendance at Sunday services and an emphasis on the benefits of community was common to all, one co-researcher mentioned the importance to her of attending a few different churches: from those who heavily feature liturgy and sung choral worship to those who are strong in preaching and providing a robust discussion of faith. She valued diversity within faith expression as part of her spirituality practice and believes no single church can "sustain all those different aspects."[8] While churches were by no means painted as perfect places by anyone, their value in sustaining faith was strongly acknowledged.

Prayer is also highlighted as vital to their faith by all co-researchers, with personal Bible study also featuring either as a fairly regular, or daily activity which inspires and challenges. Two co-researchers set aside time in the morning for Bible reading and prayer and one feels like "there is something missing" if she is too rushed to have this time before her day begins and noted that "it is interesting how it changes your day."[9] Three of the co-researchers also talked about how they feel like they are in constant conversation with God throughout the day and how while walking back from the school gate one person would describe that time "as a prayerful time in conversation with God."[10] Co-researcher E also noted how prayer functions in a church community where "prayer

7. B, "Interview."
8. D, "Interview."
9. C, "Interview."
10. B, "Interview."

requests are shared and prayers are not only for our members but for wider, global issues. It shows a little of the nature of God in caring for the deeply personal and specific, as well as the big picture."[11]

When asked about whether God was present in nature or exercise, all but one co-researcher agreed that they feel more spiritual and closer to God when in dramatic natural environments when "the majesty of nature speaks to me and calls me to worship God."[12] In addition a simply beautiful magnolia tree situated in suburbia also causes one co-researcher to "feel God's goodness in that."[13] The beauty of God's world was noted and both co-researcher C and E often felt closer to God in nature, especially by the sea listening to the waves:

> I just feel clearer in my head and heart after a time by the sea. Walking on a beach and seeing a vast expanse of sky seems to open up my heart and soul too. It seems to make room for more. More of God, more for people, more of life.[14]

While one co-researcher didn't find being in nature spiritual, she recalled her practice of using Celtic prayers as a young adult and notes that they "are based in nature and also . . . in hospitality and welcoming in people . . . they're always powerful parts of faith."[15]

Exercise was only consciously viewed as spiritual by co-researcher E who noted that she would often use walking alone in the park as an opportunity to pray or listen to podcasts of a spiritual nature. She also said that, "when we run in a group we are hearing each other's stories and witnessing our lives and I do think this is a spiritual practice."[16] However both co-researchers B and C also talked about praying while walking or hiking.

11. E, "Interview."
12. A, "Interview."
13. B, "Interview."
14. E, "Interview."
15. D, "Interview."
16. E, "Interview."

OUTWORKING OF SPIRITUALITY
AT THE SCHOOL GATE

While asking for a definition of spirituality elicited some "ums" and "ems," everyone agreed that spirituality went beyond *what* you believed, to *how* you lived your life and interacted with the people around you. Telling people what they believed at the school gate was viewed as secondary to trying in the first instance to show their faith in God by the integrity of their behavior, the tone of their interactions, and the quality of their relationships. Co-researcher D also remarked that "this is an important example for your kids as well."[17] Everyone agreed that they were open about their family's regular attendance at church and Sunday school and how that impacted decisions about kids playing Sunday sport or attending parties. They didn't hide their beliefs in that way; but in general, they didn't report many opportunities to talk to others about what they believed.

The recent Irish referenda on same-sex marriage and abortion were both viewed as very polarizing topics, with people on both sides of the arguments making a lot of assumptions about how a person of faith would vote. As a result, for anyone who intended to vote against the motions it seemed safer not to engage in any real or meaningful discussion on the topics, with this reticence based on a fear of being viewed as judgmental or lacking in compassion. Some friend groups tackled the subjects in the more focused context of a social night out, rather than at the more public school gate, and said what they really thought to closer, more trusted friends.

All co-researchers stated that they prayed regularly for friends at the school gate and sometimes even told them they were doing it! One co-researcher has noted over the years that when people pop into her head she should act on that prompting, which she believes originates from God, and phone them or send them a message. She feels that "God is leading us to help others" and that "he has used a lot of people in my life to help me in my faith . . . and

17. D, "Interview."

I feel he's also using me in other people's lives, even though I don't know exactly where and when."[18] People who were experiencing difficulties in life whether through illness, bereavement, or issues with their children were all mentioned as worthy of especial time, care, and compassion at the school gate by the co-researchers. "For me it's all about just being there for people, listening to them when they want to talk about things."[19] They also noted that when they were struggling or overwhelmed for whatever reason, people who they knew well at the school gate had shown kindness to them.

Co-researcher E believes that the sacred is either everywhere or nowhere and that in the midst of mundane exchanges about sharing lifts to hockey "are little nugget moments that are enabled by all the other interactions that make up the frame of a relationship and enable something deeper to emerge."[20] While co-researcher A admitted that in the early years at the school gate she found it difficult to be open about her faith, she is now intentionally "trying to be a bit more transparent"[21] about what she believes and as a result ended up explaining what a Bible study entailed to an interested but uninitiated parent at the side of the swimming pool. She credits this conversation "partly from knowing people better and partly from being a bit more natural with people about my faith."[22] This naturalness was something all co-researchers aimed for in their interactions.

Co-researcher D talked about her links to a group in her school called "Moms in Prayer International"[23] which gathers mums to pray for their children and their schools.[24] A core group

18. C, "Interview."

19. C, "Interview."

20. E, "Interview."

21. A, "Interview."

22. A, "Interview."

23. "Moms In Prayer International."

24. Moms in Prayer International Groups are in more than 140 countries around the world and aim to impact children and schools worldwide for Christ by gathering mothers to pray. From the 'About us' section in Moms in Prayer website: "Our vision is that every school in the world would be covered with prayer. What if you could change the world—not just for today but for

of around ten mothers have expressed interest, with three or four attending the prayer meetings at any one time. They consider any illnesses or problems they are aware of and then pray for the teachers, the children and the parents. Along with the mum who organizes the prayer group, co-researcher D is also involved in helping out at a Scripture Union Bible and outdoor activity camp for the fourth–sixth class children,[25] which is hugely popular even with the families who do not attend the Parish church.

STORIES OF ENCOUNTER

All co-researchers talked generally about being aware of God's presence in certain meaningful conversations with friends, but specific stories of encounter are worth telling.

Story One

> I had been walking in the park after school drop off on and off for a few years, occasionally with someone but mainly by myself and I frequently passed another mum from the school who was doing the same walk as me in a different direction. We started to smile and say "hello" and this went on for some time. We didn't have any children of the same age, so I had never formally met her. One day I took a risk, I stopped and asked if instead of just smiling and passing by "Would you like to walk together?" This was the start of a new friendship. A tentative relationship

---

generations to come? At Moms in Prayer International, we believe that a mom can be the single greatest force for good in the lives of her children and the children around her. We believe that lives and whole communities are changed forever when moms gather together to pray to the only One who can change a human heart. Moms can make the difference as they reach out to God in prayer—moms just like you." "Moms In Prayer International."

25. Scripture Union Youth & Schools Ministry, "Every year we work with thousands of young people in youth groups, schools and churches helping young people to understand the Christian faith in a relevant way in the changing cultural climate of 21st Century Ireland." "Scripture Union."

began with neither wanting to impose themselves on the other, but over time, as we realized that we enjoyed each other's company, we went from walking together if we turned up at the same time, to arranging to meet and letting the other know if we wouldn't be there. A rhythm emerged and terms went by, school holidays were enjoyed, and I looked forward to seeing her on our return. A few years went by and our walking twosome had grown into an occasional threesome, foursome and fivesome all from the school gate, with walking now alternated between our new venture of running. We are an odd mix of women: one of our husband's wryly commented that "Enid Blyton wouldn't have put the five of us together!" He's right, but it works. We have supported each other through a marriage breakup, the illness and subsequent deaths of parents, the difficulties of parenting, the moans, groans and laughs of everyday life and the endorphins of running in the Irish rain in November. The group matters, the support is invaluable, and I have learnt that by being vulnerable and sharing my grief, my anger and my hurt over the years, I have enabled others to share theirs with me.[26]

Story Two

I was sitting at the school gate in a new friend's car and having asked her how she was, she burst into tears and told me . . . about her dad, completely out of the blue. Actually, that morning I had been thinking of her and thought I had to go and say hello to her, so I felt I was led just to talk to her and . . . I really only listened, I didn't have advice, I couldn't do anything to make things better . . . but she told me about it and I said I'll be thinking of her, I'll pray for her and she told me about a month later that she'd never been able to tell anyone about that and that it meant a lot that I was there on the day. I feel God was in that. He made me think of her that day and I often

26. E, "Interview."

try and fix things for people and give some advice and I
didn't that day. I think I just knew she needed to talk and
there was nothing else I needed to do. I do think God
helped me to just keep quiet and listen . . . and give a hug
in the end.[27]

Story Three

Walking in the park one morning I passed another mum
who is not a close friend, but who I have known for many
years. One of her best friends who I also knew, had died
from cancer the previous week and this was the first time
I had seen her since then. She was out walking her dog
wearing headphones, a baseball cap and dark glasses and
looking for all the world like she wanted to be left alone
in her grief. We passed by and said "hello." My heart
contracted at her pain. I prayed for her as I continued
walking. I came to a fork in the paths and decided to take
a different route, so that I might pass her again. I did and
this time I felt I should stop and speak. "I just wanted to
give you a hug and say how sorry I am about X, I understand if you don't want to talk." We hugged and she said,
"Thank you I feel so awful, but no, you're different I'll
talk to you." We had a brief chat about our disbelief that
X was gone and went our separate ways.[28]

Story Four

I was chatting in the car with my friend whose husband
died from cancer just a year ago. She was telling me about
how her kids were coping with big exams in the midst
of their grief and how her dog, which had been a gift
from her husband was sick, and then; just at the point
we were getting out to pick up our kids, she admitted she

27. C, "Interview."
28. E, "Interview."

was dreading the next day because she had to go in to her husband's workplace to receive a book of memories for the family from his former colleagues. I acknowledged that this would be a difficult and upsetting experience and we parted company. I came away and thought about how much she had to deal with on her own and realized that of all of it, the memorial was foremost in her mind. The next day I was chatting with other mums at the gate and I saw her coming straight towards me, her face pale and drawn. Remembering where she had just come from, I left my conversation mid-sentence, went towards her and just hugged her. I told her I was so sorry, that it must have been so hard. She nodded and fled back to the safety of her children and car.[29]

COMMUNICATION

While everyone is part of WhatsApp and texting groups in their school context for information dissemination, all, except one co-researcher, were enthusiastic about the value of sending texts in between verbal communication with friends at the school gate:

> I find texts really useful to let people know that I'm praying for them or just to check up on how people are if I don't see them or sometimes at the school gate you don't really get a chance to have a deep conversation with people, it can be a bit superficial, it just depends on how many people are around at the time. So just maybe to follow up on something that we've talked about, a throwaway comment and then ask whatever happened about that thing?[30]

Co-researcher B who also values the ongoing combination of one to one conversation and texting said, "I think if you've been open and actually texting and communicating in the times you're not seeing each other, its easier then to have a deeper and more

29. E, "Interview."
30. A, "Interview."

real conversation when you do see them."[31] Co-researcher A said, "sometimes you can also be a bit more courageous by text than you would be in person, in the way you phrase things and you can edit yourself more."[32] In sensitive situations where someone has been bereaved, for example, co-researcher C will start with a message, "because they might not have time to answer a call or want to talk." She often prefaces these messages with "I don't expect a reply" and continues to follow up as she has been told that "it has meant a lot to [her friend] to know there is someone there praying for her and thinking of her."[33]

The sometimes inflammatory nature of group chats was acknowledged and co-researcher A uses the medium to try and steer those conversations to a more positive and encouraging outcome.[34] Researcher E believes "texting builds connections and strengthens relationships . . . but there is of course a problem with tone on text and sometimes it takes real conversation to clear up any misunderstandings arising from a text!"[35] This lack of tone is what is off-putting about text communication to co-researcher D, and she much prefers to talk in person.

PERCEIVED IMPACTS OF SPIRITUALITY AT THE SCHOOL GATE

Concluding remarks in the interviews about school gate spirituality revealed the following. Co-researcher A said that it has been interesting developing relationships through her daughter and

31. B, "Interview."

32. A, "Interview."

33. C, "Interview."

34. One example given by a co-researcher about potentially inflammatory group chat was a parent becoming agitated about the amount of homework given by a particular teacher. This parent was trying to drum up support for an organized approach to the school using the class WhatsApp. The co-researcher, as a former teacher, then used the chat to explain the educative purpose of homework for children and diffused the situation.

35. E, "Interview."

to have the opportunity to meet a lot of people who have different life experiences. She saw the value of showing how what you believe impacts your life choices such as what you spend your time or money on. She highlighted trying to be a positive influence within the school and of trying to set an example in how she conducts herself in relationships. She recognizes that now her daughter is older she is infrequently at the school and regrets this change, but realizes she needs to be more intentional in her interactions as a result.

Co-researcher B saw the importance of spirituality at the school gate and the integration of "who you are in your personal faith, personal life, church life and your everyday life and how they can't be separated." She believes because of her faith she cares about the people at school at a deeper level, "there is an awareness of trying to care about them as God sees them and praying for the things they're struggling with, so I think there is a spiritual element to the everyday encounters."[36]

Co-researcher C recognized that she had talked a lot about relationships in her interview and how she feels God uses her in these relationships by listening, by sending text messages or by doing practical things like bringing children home from school if their mother is unable to due to illness or bereavement. For her it has made a big difference when people pray for her; therefore she prays for a lot of friends and said "I think everyone wants to know there's someone thinking of them."[37] She feels God has used people at the school gate in her life and so wants to be open to how God can use her in other people's lives.

Co-researcher D also focused on relationships and how you need to put time and effort into them at the school gate. As someone who has both been a full-time stay-at-home mum and a working mum she could really see the difference in the two experiences and how it makes a difference both to the children and the quality of relationships formed between parents.

36. B, "Interview."
37. C, "Interview."

Co-researcher E has long been intentional in bringing her whole self to the school gate and sees her spirituality as relational on every level. For her, like co-researcher B it is based on God's love for her and how that has to spill over to those around her: "Love the Lord your God with all your heart and love your neighbor as yourself."[38]

38. E, "Interview."

Discussion and Conclusion

INTRODUCTION

This exploratory research sought to establish if mothers who are intentionally spiritually engaged found that it made a difference to relationships they made at the primary school gate. The findings strongly suggest that the co-researchers have each, in their different Anglican school environments, been a positive, compassionate, caring influence and have therefore to some degree modeled the "framework for fruitfulness" as advocated by Mark Greene[1] in the expression and practice of their spirituality. Within these four schools most parents do not profess to have a personal faith, but appear respectful of and open to the co-researchers who display their faith in their everyday interactions and actions.

Where intentionality was especially present, concern and prayer for others was the chief outcome of the co-researchers' spirituality, alongside offers of practical assistance. Viewing people as God views them, which to one co-researcher meant with love and compassion, was the embodied way in which everyday encounters were perceived as spiritual encounters. Each of the co-researchers was aware of the mystery of God's spirit within us, the mystery that leads us to someone's car at the school gate or to what Carl McColman calls a "thin place" which is "recognized through intuition, through feeling, through attentiveness to silence and the subtle

---

1. Greene lists, "Model godly character, make good work, minister grace and love, mould culture, be a mouthpiece for truth and justice and be a messenger of the gospel." Greene, *Fruitfulness*, 35.

knowing of the human body."[2] An acceptance of the presence of God in the everyday by the co-researchers allowed them to, in some, but not all instances, sense a closeness to the spiritual realm at the school gate. The findings display examples of compassion in all of the co-researchers' narratives and thus validate the starting point of this heuristic inquiry which sought to "consciously include the researcher's own experience within the framework of the study . . . and acknowledge the particular features of spiritual experience which she personally finds to be significant."[3]

IMPLICATIONS OF THE FINDINGS

The findings of this study point primarily to the fact that spirituality at the school gate is relational in nature. Each of the co-researchers have, in the first instance a living, active relationship with God that is nourished by private prayer and the study of Scripture and spiritual books; but is also sustained by community through their church and small group attendance. Emanating from this relationship with the Divine is an understanding that their spirituality is not restricted to a two-way vertical relationship, but rather with the aid of the Holy Spirit will flow in all directions permeating the relationships with those around them, including the people they encounter at the school gate. I would suggest that authenticity is a useful way to describe the nature of this relational spirituality and point to Michael O'Sullivan who wrote, "spirituality studies the dynamic spirit of authenticity in human subjectivity and the extent to which it is, or is not, lived out faithfully in lived experience."[4] The findings suggest that when a person of faith authentically integrates their faith into their lived experience, then positive relational transformation occurs. Co-researcher A recognized that earlier in her school gate experience she had been behaving in a dichotomous way:

2. McColman, "Thin Places."
3. Flanagan, "Liberty God," 73.
4. O'Sullivan, "The Turn to Spirituality."

> I felt like I wasn't really being true to myself that I would talk about different things with Christians and non-Christians and now I'm trying to be a bit more transparent . . . and partly it's from knowing people better and partly from like, actually genuinely trying to be a bit more natural with people about my faith.[5]

Going on to tell a story about sitting at the swimming pool and sharing with another parent how she engages in the faith-based practice of small group Bible study demonstrated how this was now occurring more naturally in her life.

Alongside authenticity, which encourages integrated spirituality and leads to natural Spirit-filled encounters, the importance of time (and repeated times) cannot be overlooked. The school gate is a unique site of repeated micro-engagements over a long number of years and if parents have the time(s) to invest in building relationships, they are positioned within a unique stage of their life to maximize this opportunity. The data show that working full-time means less contact time, and there is a need for intentionality in order to relate to other parents on a deeper level than a wave from a car window. Small interactions lead to conversations, which can lead to friendships, which will lead to mutual support, which will lead to growth and spiritual flourishing. These are bold claims but ones to which the data attest: "the group matters, the support is invaluable, and I have learnt that by being vulnerable and sharing my grief, my anger and my hurt over the years, I have enabled others to share theirs with me."[6]

The findings show that if time and intentionality are employed then authentic, relational spirituality does lead to enhanced relationships, which leads to a more positive school gate community and friendships that are rooted and will outlast the years spent together at the school.

5. A, "Interview."
6. E, "Interview."

IDENTIFICATION OF EXPECTED
AND UNEXPECTED FINDINGS

The presence of some degree of spirituality at the school gate was assumed from the purposive sample of co-researchers. This was due to their vibrant faith couched in their church environment; but the extent to which they identified the secular school gate as a place where spirituality could emerge, and the amount of intentionality employed, was unclear at the beginning of the research process. There was a recognition from two co-researchers that people who do not claim to have faith in God do of course also behave in a compassionate, caring way to their friends and acquaintances at the school gate. While this was noted as positive by the co-researchers, the reasons for this were not reflected upon within the scope of the interviews.

The presence of a "Moms in Prayer" group in one school was noteworthy and unexpected. While the organization is American in origin, it now operates in more than 140 countries worldwide including Ireland and neighboring United Kingdom. Its presence in a faith-based Protestant school in Ireland is however not a given, and seemed to rely upon a proactive mother, who was aware of its existence and instigated a prayer group. The international website does not list numbers on how many Irish schools have links to the organization, but states that groups commit to an hour of prayer a week for children and schools.[7]

DISCUSSION OF THE FINDINGS IN
RELATION TO THE LITERATURE

The study belongs firmly in the field of lived or everyday religion, which "draws attention to the lived expression of a spirituality in people's everyday lives."[8] While Ammerman and McGuire discovered in their studies, that in varying degrees, faith does emerge

7. "Moms In Prayer International."

8. Flanagan and O'Sullivan, "Spirituality in Contemporary Ireland," 55–73.

in everyday lives and discovered this through "practices and narratives more than tightly argued philosophical systems,"[9] they focused primarily on workplace and personal, home-based practices of spirituality. I would argue that the school gate is a unique, (mostly) secular social context, that is neither a defined workplace nor an arena of leisure activities. It is an intersectional social space, which exists over a long period of time and is linked directly to motherhood and parenting.

Wolfteich and Flanagan have both pointed to the paucity of spirituality scholarship on the subject of women, with Wolfteich focusing on motherhood and suggesting that life writing could open up a view of "concrete, everyday practices of mothering as experienced not by celibate elders but by laywomen embedded in the day-to-day care of children."[10] The data presented here, while not life writing, sheds much needed light on the concrete, everyday practice of showing up at the school gate daily, weekly, monthly, yearly with an embodied faith that is expressed relationally with other mothers and fathers.

There is a richness in the stories told by the co-researchers, stories that they had not in some cases identified as relational spiritual encounters, but during the interview process, recognized that they were. Ammerman speaks eloquently to this "modest" spirituality in ordinary life when she writes:

> To call a story a "spiritual narrative" is simply to recognize that something about it concerns the life of the spirit and the communities of discourse in which spiritual traditions are made real. The spirituality we are listening for . . . is a more modest, but nonetheless profound recognition that the world is not wholly a story that can be empirically told. There is another layer of consciousness that can weave, more or less pervasively, in and out of ordinary events.[11]

---

9. Ammerman, *Sacred Stories*, 6.

10. Wolfteich, "Spirituality, Mothering, and Public Leadership," 146.

11. Ammerman, *Sacred Stories*, 9.

I would suggest that both the findings and the literature point to the fact that it is very important for people to actively reflect on their contexts of encounter at every stage of life; but the nature of the school gate, because of its repetitive regularity, can perhaps dull one into thinking it is of little significance. It can also feel interminable in its time span, but in reality, it has a limit imposed by the relentless, yet somehow surprising aging of our children. The school gate as a locus of community also has an intrinsic value when viewed through the lens of a lived, authentic, dynamic spirituality which the data has shown can, and does, positively influence relationships. Overall the literature of everyday religion was extremely useful as a background to this study as it gave academic validation to the presence of spirituality in this seemingly mundane setting. However, no direct comparisons could be made as neither Ammerman nor McGuire looked at the school gates as a specific context.[12]

The reflection-based books referred to in this study were of benefit in terms of highlighting the value of action stemming from spiritual reflection. The data corroborated what Schell found at her turquoise table: "[women] are drawn to each other and our stories and through that experience oneness. It's how community is built: layer by layer, struggle by struggle, story by story."[13] For the running group that co-researcher E is part of, this is exactly how their community was built. In *Holy Spokes*[14] Everett found that love and concern for our neighbor results in better communities and Schell wanted to "make a place where we all feel comfortable and safe"[15] at her turquoise table. Narratives in the data show that if embodied spirituality is intentionally present at a school gate then even those who are grieving and hurting can show up and find both a community and a safe place in the embodied form of an attentive listener.

---

12. Other relevant works in the field of everyday religion are: Taylor, *Altar in the World*; Slee, Porter, and Phillips, *Faith Lives of Women*.

13. Schell, *Turquoise Table*, 77.

14. Everett, *Holy Spokes*.

15. Schell, *Turquoise Table*, 124.

STRENGTHS AND LIMITATIONS OF THE STUDY

Situated within the field of everyday religion, a major strength of the study is its innovative focus on the school gate. It is surprising that as a context it has hitherto been overlooked, unlike the workplace for example, which has received a lot of attention in the academy of spirituality.[16] I would suggest that this is due to continued societal focus on the importance of the workplace as the chief component of the quest for gender equality. While equality in employment opportunities and salaries has been a feminist aim for decades, women with families are still struggling to succeed in academia compared to their male colleagues.[17] I would argue that representation of the whole spectrum of women's lives in academic writing, from "elite" to "everyday," is also vital to the advancement of feminism.

Since the rise of women's rights, women have been told that they can have it all: education, a career, a husband (or wife), and a family. The data show that middle-class women who are currently parenting in their mid-life struggle to manage all of this supposed recipe for success, and have sometimes chosen to make sacrificial financial decisions in order to stay at home with their young children. One co-researcher who worked part-time in the mornings noted that full-time work entailed the need for after-school services and not being able to attend sports days or to get to know other parents.[18] One strength of this study is that it is casting a targeted beam of light on a realm of mothers' lives that is undervalued by society as a whole and is therefore also unnoticed by the academy.

16. Giacalone and Jurkiewicz, *Handbook of Workplace Spirituality and Organizational Performance*; Burack, "Spirituality in the Workplace"; Krishnakumar and Neck, "Spirituality in the Workplace."

17. See for example, "Gender inequality in higher education is an internationally observed issue. Women continue to be 'vastly under-represented in top positions within the higher education sector' as well as in 'top academic decision-making positions' across Europe." HEA, "Gender Equality in Irish Higher Education," 7.

18. C, "Interview."

The chief limitation of the study is the narrowness of its scope and its sole representation of a minority section of the Irish population. The most recent census undertaken in Ireland was in 2016 and recorded that "the percentage of the population who identified as Catholic on the census has fallen sharply from 84.2 percent in 2011 to 78.3 percent in 2016."[19] The population who identify as Church of Ireland remained constant at 3 percent. Many schools in Ireland, especially in larger towns and cities, are now strongly multi-cultural and an analysis of spirituality in this context would provide a broader picture. The study was based solely in middle-class Dublin and it is acknowledged that including rural settings would also harvest more diverse experiences. The presence of social concerns and activism at the school gate could also be probed more deeply as a facet of spirituality, as only the topics of same-sex marriage and abortion were touched on in the interviews. The analysis, while rich in content is therefore particular and not representative of all school gate spirituality.

Furthermore the study did not explore the experiences of fathers at the school gate. All the female co-researchers did mention the presence of fathers in passing, but the only story told about deepening relationships was between a widowed father and other fathers from his children's class, who had reached out to him socially. Mothers did however also contribute practically to this difficult situation by offering lifts to afterschool activities. On the whole, perhaps for reasons of propriety, there was little discussion about fathers being part of the female co-researchers' supportive friend groups.

FURTHER AREAS OF RESEARCH

This study has added to existing knowledge of everyday religion by developing a view of mothers and their everyday spiritual lives within the context of a contextualized and culturally specific school gate community. As previously mentioned, this context

19. Central Statistics Office, "Census 2016," 72.

has hitherto been unidentified as a site of spiritual engagement, because it has been undervalued, and therefore overlooked. Nevertheless, there are obvious extensions to this research in the Irish context alone, with Catholic-run schools being the main provider of primary education in the state (90 percent). As a non-denominational education provider, Educate Together aims to provide "long-overdue choice of equality-based primary and second-level schools for thousands of families in Ireland" and guarantees "equality of access and esteem to students irrespective of their social, cultural or religious background."[20] The rise in demand for non-denominational schools reflects both the fact that the fastest growing religions in Ireland are Orthodox, Hindu, and Muslim and that there is a marked rise since the 2011 census in the number who consider themselves to have "no religion," who now account for just under 10 percent of the population (9.8 percent).[21]

The study should therefore be viewed as a starting point for a wider treatment of the topic, as it provides insightful evidence of the impact spirituality at the school gate can have on relationships and shines a light on a much under-researched section of the population, namely mothers and their experiences. Further aspects of mothers' experiences that might be explored are: sports days, birthday parties, musical and dramatic performances, and other extra-curricular activities.

RECOMMENDATIONS FOR PRACTICE IN LIGHT OF THE FINDINGS

In highlighting the importance of women's spiritual autobiographies to the field of spirituality Bernadette Flanagan surmised that these spiritual narratives are "resources of empowerment and guidance for present and future generations of women."[22] I would hope that in the first instance the findings of this study would encourage

20. "Educate Together."
21. "Census 2016."
22. Flanagan, "Women and Spirituality," 335.

scholars of spirituality to take note of the school gate as a locus of spiritual community and invest in it with further research.

Perhaps more importantly, I would hope that mothers themselves would recognize that if they are spiritually aware (love God), then the school gate provides abounding opportunities for loving community (love thy neighbor). The period of life that corresponds with parenting and attending the school gate is one that, for most people in Ireland (and Europe), now matches mid-life rather than early adulthood, due to most women choosing to start a family in their thirties rather than their twenties.[23] I highlight this because for those for whom spirituality is of primary importance, the period of mid-life which is a miasma of caring for aging parents, parenting young children, and working to pay the bills, may correspond with entering into what Rohr in *Falling Upward* calls the "second half of life."[24] He suggests that "there are two halves of life with significantly different tasks. If you get your 'container' in the first half of life, then you are ready for the 'contents' that the container was meant to hold."[25]

In my opinion one of the most important spiritual "contents" we hold in our container of life is relationality, as modeled most effectively in the Trinity. Once the sleep-deprived, home-centered years have passed and the busy years of school activities and friendships for children and parents begin in earnest, mid-life seems like a never-ending rollercoaster. However, the co-researchers who are nearing the end of the "school gate ride" attest to the fact that we only gain perspective on seasons of life when we reflect on them as they are nearing their end, or are already over. While the data described a busyness that also involved self-sacrifice in order to be present during the primary school years, the co-researchers were also grateful for the richness of these years, when children still

23. New Central Statistics Office data revealed that on average, mothers are giving birth to their first child at almost thirty-one years of age. Three decades ago, women were almost five years younger when they had their first baby. "Quarter 2 2019."

24. Rohr, *Falling Upward*.

25. Rohr, *Immortal Diamond*, 216.

crucially need (and want) their parents' input and involvement. I would therefore encourage parents to be spiritually engaged and self-reflective, and to view the extended period spent at the school gate as a wonderful opportunity to authentically live out their spirituality in a dynamic, relational way.

CONCLUSION

This exploratory, heuristic study sought to establish whether spirituality enhanced relationships made at the school gate. As Clark Moustakas stated, "in heuristic research the investigator must have had a direct, personal encounter with the phenomenon being investigated,"[26] and from the researcher's personal experience at the school gate, a heuristic journey began. Moustakas suggests that at the start of the process comes an invitation from the researcher's consciousness that "represents an invitation for further elucidation,"[27] and in the case of this study it was the image of the Sacred Heart of Jesus, which seeming to embody both suffering and compassion, cast new light on the existing knowledge of the researcher. The data provided numerous examples of embodied, integrated spirituality at the school gate and many of them held suffering and compassion at their core. The co-researchers credited this as stemming from their active relationship with God made manifest by regular prayer, study of the Bible, church fellowship, and community. All attest to the fact that they love God and, to the best of their abilities, love their neighbor. Elizabeth Barrett Browning reminded us that:

> Earth's crammed with heaven,
> And every common bush afire with God,
> But only he who sees takes off his shoes;
> The rest sit round and pluck blackberries, . . .[28]

26. Moustakas, *Heuristic Research*, 14.
27. Moustakas, *Heuristic Research*, 10.
28. Browning, "Aurora Leigh."

The school gate is part of this earth crammed with heaven, but we have to pause awhile, take off our shoes and notice the presence of God there, mindful that some of those around us remain unaware that the liminal, thin spaces of God can appear anywhere.

Appendix

INTERVIEW PROMPT SHEET

Section 1: Introduction and Basic Personal Information

Introductory comments to welcome co-researcher and introduce the topic of school gate spirituality—how mothers of Christian faith experience, express, and practice their spirituality in the everyday location of the school gate.

- Where and in what year were you born?
- How long have you been living in Dublin?
- What is your highest level of formal education?
- What sector did you work in before having children?
- Do you work outside the home now? Tell me about that.

Section 2: Information About Your National School

- How many children do you have, or have had in national school?
- Do you pick up your child/children using a car or do you go on foot/by bicycle?

- Can you tell me about the location or layout of your school gate? For example is it conducive to parents being able to chat to each other before the children are released back to their parents' care?

- Is there a café or park nearby that you and other parents habitually meet in?

- Do you have class reps who organize social nights and have you attended these gatherings?

- Would you say your school has a high proportion of stay-at-home mothers or fathers or are there a lot of grandparents/after-school staff who collect from school?

- If so, do you think this has any impact on the relationships made at the school gate?

- Are there after-school activities like sport that parents are also involved in? If so, does this promote relationship building?

- In your opinion, does your school actively promote its Church of Ireland ethos? If so, can you tell me some ways in which this happens?

Section 3: Your Personal Faith

- Do you regularly attend a religious institution? In what ways does it sustain your spiritual life?

- What do you understand by the term Christian spirituality?

- Are you part of a religious small group? What is its function?

- Tell me about any spiritual practices you have such as prayer or reading Scripture. How do you feel they inform your interactions at the school gate?

- Do you maintain any other spiritual practices that are not part of your established faith tradition (meditation or centering prayer, for example)?

- How do you feel about demonstrating your spirituality to others outside of your close friends and family?

- Do you ever think of exercise or being in nature as spiritual? Tell me about that.

Section 4: School Gate Spirituality

- Are your closer school gate friendships with people of faith or of no discernible faith?

- Do you feel like any of the everyday encounters you have at the school gate have a spiritual element? If not, why not?

- *If above answer was affirmative follow on with this:* Can you describe to me an occasion when you felt God was very much present in a conversation at the school gate—what was different about that conversation?

- During this time as a parent of school-going children have *you* faced a particularly difficult time, like the death of someone close to you or an illness? Have any relationships made at the school gate sustained you? Can you tell me about that?

- On the other hand, have you supported friends through a difficult period in their life? What role, if any, did your spirituality play in this?

- Have you any (other) stories of deepening spiritual encounter with people as your relationships have grown over the years?

- Do you find texting/WhatsApp a useful way to support friends at the school gate? Do you find you communicate more freely in person or by text?

- Did recent referenda in Ireland on same-sex marriage and the legalization of abortion lead you into any conversations of a spiritual nature?

- To finish, is there anything else that you'd like to tell me that we haven't touched on in our conversation so far?

Bibliography

A, Co-researcher. "Interview." 2019.

Abraham, Leah. "You Are An Immaculate Measure of Grace." *She Loves Magazine* (2019). https://shelovesmagazine.com/2019/you-are-an-immaculate-measure-of-grace/.

Ahlgren, Gillian T. W. *The Tenderness of God: Reclaiming Our Humanity.* Minneapolis: Fortress, 2017.

Ammerman, Nancy Tatom. *Sacred Stories, Spiritual Tribes: Finding Religion in Everyday Life.* Oxford: Oxford University Press, 2014.

Autobiography of Blessed Mary of the Divine Heart. Lisbon: Religious of the Good Shepherd, 1993.

B, Co-researcher. "Interview." 2019.

Browning, Elizabeth Barrett. "Aurora Leigh: A Poem." https://digital.library.upenn.edu/women/barrett/aurora/aurora.html.

Burack, Elmer H. "Spirituality in the Workplace." *Journal of Organizational Change Management* 12, no. 4 (August 12, 1999): 280–92.

C, Co-researcher. "Interview." 2019.

Central Statistics Office. "Census 2016." Cork, Ireland, 2016. www.cso.ie.

———. "Vital Statistics: Quarter 2 2019." Cork, Ireland, 2019. www.cso.ie.

D, Co-researcher. "Interview." 2019.

E, Co-researcher. "Interview." 2019.

"Educate Together." www.educatetogether.ie.

Everett, Laura. *Holy Spokes: The Search for Urban Spirituality on Two Wheels.* Grand Rapids: Eerdmans, 2017.

Fincher, Dale, and Jonalyn Grace Fincher. *Coffee Shop Conversations: Making the Most of Spiritual Small Talk.* Grand Rapids: Zondervan, 2010.

Flanagan, Bernadette. "Liberty God: A Heuristic Study of Irish Urban Spirituality in Dublin's Liberties." Milltown Institute, Dublin, 1998.

———. "Quaestio Divina." *The Way* 53, no. 4 (2014): 126–36.

———. "Women and Spirituality." In *The Bloomsbury Guide to Christian Spirituality*, edited by Richard Woods and Peter Tyler, 329–337. London: Bloomsbury, 2012.

Flanagan, Bernadette, and Michael O'Sullivan. "Spirituality in Contemporary Ireland: Manifesting Indigeneity." *Spiritus: A Journal of Christian Spirituality* 16, no. 2A (2016): 55–73. doi:10.1353/scs.2016.0051.

Foddy, William H. *Constructing Questions for Interviews and Questionnaires: Theory and Practice in Social Research.* Cambridge: Cambridge University Press, 1993.

Ganiel, Gladys. *Evangelicalism and Conflict in Northern Ireland.* New York: Palgrave Macmillan, 2008.

Giacalone, Robert A., and Carole L. Jurkiewicz. *Handbook of Workplace Spirituality and Organizational Performance.* New York: M. E. Sharpe, 2003.

Greene, Mark. *Fruitfulness on the Frontline: Making a Difference Where You Are.* Nottingham: InterVarsity, 2014.

HEA. "HEA National Review of Gender Equality in Irish Higher Education Institutions." Dublin, 2016. www.hea.ie.

Holy Bible: New International Version. Hodder & Stoughton, 2011.

Ivtzan, Itai, et al. "Linking Religion and Spirituality with Psychological Well-Being: Examining Self-Actualisation, Meaning in Life, and Personal Growth Initiative." *Journal of Religion and Health* 52, no. 3 (2013): 915–29.

"Jen Hatmaker." www.jenhatmaker.com.

Kidd, Sue Monk. *Firstlight: The Early Inspirational Writings of Sue Monk Kidd.* London: Penguin, 2006.

Krishnakumar, Sukumarakurup, and Christopher P. Neck. "The 'What', 'Why' and 'How' of Spirituality in the Workplace." *Journal of Managerial Psychology* 17, no. 3 (May 12, 2002): 153–64. doi:10.1108/02683940210423060.

Kumar, Ranjit. *Research Methodology: A Step-by-Step Guide for Beginners.* London: SAGE, 2011.

"The London Institute for Contemporary Christianity." www.licc.org.uk.

McColman, Carl. "Thin Places, Contemplation, and Discernment: A Few Questions About Celtic Spirituality." https://carlmccolman.com/thin-places-contemplation-and-discernment/.

McGuire, Meredith B. *Lived Religion: Faith and Practice in Everyday Life.* Oxford: Oxford University Press, 2008.

"Moms In Prayer International." https://momsinprayer.org.

Moustakas, Clark E. *Heuristic Research: Design, Methodology, and Applications.* London: SAGE, 1990.

Newell, Robert, and Philip Burnard. *Research for Evidence-Based Practice in Healthcare.* 2nd ed. Chichester: Wiley-Blackwell, 2011.

O'Sullivan, Michael. "The Turn to Spirituality." Unpublished lecture delivered in the Spirituality Matters series of public lectures at All Hallows College, Dublin City University, November 9, 2010.

Patterson, Ruth. *The Gaze of Love.* Dublin: Veritas, 2016.

Rohr, Richard. *Falling Upward.* San Francisco: Jossey-Bass, 2011.

———. *Immortal Diamond: The Search for Our True Self.* London: SPCK, 2013.

Rossall, Judith. "Reform Spirituality: Calvin." In *The Bloomsbury Guide to Christian Spirituality*, edited by Richard Woods and Peter Tyler, 139–46. London: Bloomsbury, 2012.

Schell, Kristin. *The Turquoise Table: Finding Community and Connection in Your Own Front Yard*. Nashville: Thomas Nelson, 2017.

Schneiders, Sandra M. "Biblical Spirituality." *Interpretation: A Journal of Bible and Theology* 70, no. 4 (October 16, 2016): 417–30.

"Scripture Union." www.scriptureunion.ie.

Sheldrake, Philip. *Explorations in Spirituality: History, Theology, and Social Practice*. New York: Paulist, 2010.

———. "Michel de Certeau: Spirituality and The Practice of Everyday Life." *Spiritus: A Journal of Christian Spirituality* 12, no. 2 (2012): 207–16. doi:10.1353/scs.2012.0024.

Silverman, David. *Doing Qualitative Research: A Practical Handbook*. London: SAGE, 2010.

Slee, Nicola, Fran Porter, and Anne Phillips. *The Faith Lives of Women and Girls: Qualitative Research Perspectives*. Routledge, 2016.

Taylor, Barbara Brown. *An Altar in the World: Finding the Sacred Beneath Our Feet*. Norwich: Canterbury, 2017.

Tickner, Nicola. "Interesting Facts—First Look at Data from POD, 2016/2017." https://www.education.ie/en/Publications/Statistics/Primary-Online-Database-POD-/POD-Interesting-Facts-First-Look-at-Data-from-POD-2016–2017.pdf.

Waaijman, Kees. *Spirituality: Forms, Foundations, Methods*. Peeters, 2002.

Wolfteich, Claire E. "Practices of 'Unsaying': Michel de Certeau, Spirituality Studies, and Practical Theology." *Spiritus: A Journal of Christian Spirituality* 12, no. 2 (2012): 161–71. doi:10.1353/scs.2012.0031.

———. "Spirituality, Mothering, and Public Leadership: Women's Life Writing and Generative Directions for Spirituality Studies." *Spiritus: A Journal of Christian Spirituality* 17, no. 2 (2017): 145–64. doi:10.1353/scs.2017.0024.

Lightning Source UK Ltd.
Milton Keynes UK
UKHW020652170420
361845UK00005B/48